C0-EJG-415

The People's Church
A Defense of My Church

The People's Church

A Defense of My Church

by
Bonaventure Kloppenburg O.F.M.

Translated
by
Matthew J. O'Connell

FRANCISCAN HERALD PRESS
1434 West 51st Street • Chicago, Illinois 60609

The People's Church by Bonaventure Kloppenburg O.F.M., translated by Matthew J. O'Connell from the Spanish *Iglesia Popular,* Ediciones Paulinas, 1977.

Library of Congress Cataloging in Publication Data

Kloppenburg, Bonaventure, 1919-
The people's church.

Translation of Iglesia popular.
Includes bibliographical references.
1. Liberation theology. 2. Socialism and Catholic Church. I. Title.
BT83.57.K5413 261.8 77-26303
ISBN 0-8199-0692-1

Published with Ecclesiastical Approval

MADE IN THE UNITED STATES OF AMERICA

Abbreviations

Abbott: *The Documents of Vatican II,* edited by Walter M. Abbott S.J. (New York: Herder and Herder & Association Press, 1966). *AG* 26c/616, = *Ad Gentes,* no. 26, paragraph 3, p. 616, in Abbott. The documents quoted in this book are

- *AG:* *Ad Gentes:* Decree on the Church's Missionary Activity
- *DV:* *Dei Verbum:* Dogmatic Constitution on Divine Revelation
- *DH:* *Dignitatis Humanae:* Declaration on Religious Freedom
- *GS:* *Gaudium et Spes:* Pastoral Constitution on the Church in the Modern World
- *LG:* *Lumen Gentium:* Dogmatic Constitution on the Church
- *PO:* *Presbyterorum Ordinis:* Decree on the Ministry and Life of Priests
- *SC:* *Sacrosanctum Concilium:* Constitution on the Sacred Liturgy
- *UR:* *Unitatis Redintegratio:* Decree on Ecumenism

OTHER FREQUENTLY USED DOCUMENTS INCLUDE

DS: Henry Denzinger and Adolf Schönmetzer (eds.), *Enchiridion symbolorum* (32nd ed.; Freiburg: Herder, 1963).

PL: *Patrologia Latina.* Edited by J.-P. Migne. Paris, 1844-64

TPS: The Pope Speaks. Washington, D.C., 1954—

SCRIPTURE IS QUOTED FROM THE *New American Bible,*
EXCEPT WHERE OTHERWISE INDICATED
(*JB* = *The Jerusalem Bible*)

Prefatory Note

Apologetics, they say, is outdated. Would that it were! For, if the defense of the Christian faith were no longer needed, it would mean that the faith was no longer being attacked or denied or falsified or changed. Yet nowadays we who identify ourselves with the "institutional" Church (is there really any other?) and love it and dedicate ourselves to it, have the impression that others not only want to "purify" and "renew" us (that was one of the great aims of the Second Vatican Council) but go further and seek to change the Church totally.

In this Report we shall be dealing with groups and individuals whose professed aim is to promote an ideological struggle within the Church and thereby to "deideologize" and "reinterpret" the Christian faith, to effect a rereading of the Bible, to liberate the conscience of the masses, to appropriate the liturgy for themselves and by all these means create a new "Church of the People." To attain their goal, they inveigh against our holy Church, attack its highest authorities, heap scorn on its theologians, and reject its institutions. Their literary approach is the quarrel, the accusation, the insult, the attack. Our study and critique of their options, positions, aims, methods, and slogans is conditioned by the literary approach they themselves have chosen. Without our having intended it, this Report has turned into a short *Apologia pro ecclesia mea,* a defense of my Church.

— The Author

Preface

The sixteenth annual meeting of the Conference of Latin American Bishops (CELAM) was held in Puerto Rico during December of 1976. With an eye both to evangelization and to the upcoming Third General Conference of Latin American Bishops (announced for 1978), the bishops urged the deeper "study of the *Iglesia Popular* and other theologico-ideological phenomena of the same kind."

In recent years, a large number of documents, articles, and books have been telling us in an increasingly emphatic tone of voice of the need for a "Church of the People" or "of the poor" or "of and for the people" — a Church that will be "born of the people," a Church that will be a "class Church" and thus new and different from the "official Church" that is institutional and embraces all classes. This "new Church" will provide "a new alternative type of ecclesial life."

According to these sources, everything will have to be "new" in the desired "Church of the People." Catchwords like "new Christianity," "new Church," "new faith," "new ministries," and "new spirituality" recur constantly in these writings.

At the Conferences of Latin American Theologians in Mexico City in August 1975, Jon Sobrino S.J. explained the "new faith" thus: "What is meant is not that we will understand the old faith in a different way, but that a new practice will give rise to a new faith."[1] Or in the words, some months earlier, of the final statement of the Second International Convention of Christians for Socialism (Quebec, April 1975): "The people of God are now reclaiming the Scriptures and reading them once again from the viewpoint of the poor and the oppressed classes. Moreover, they are claiming the responsibility for deciding on their own the course of action within the Church. Finally, they are once again making their own the liturgical and sacramental symbols, and striking out on new paths of contemplation, celebration, and Eucharist that will lead them both to fidelity to Christ and to the struggle for the liberation of the poor."[2]

The following pages are a detailed investigation into what this new "Church of the People" is or claims to be. Our study has three parts.

Contents

The People's Church

A Defense of My Church

I. Generalities

Since the idea of the "Church of the People" has arisen in the context of the Christians for Socialism (CfS) movement, we shall first study the chief documents and spokesmen of this movement; then we shall examine the documents of the related movements that are now proliferating throughout Latin America.

The documents on which this study is based are given in the following list. Later references to them will be by their number in this list and by their internal divisions or pages of the books in which they have been reprinted (e.g., 4/I, 1, 13, or 7/p. 457).

1. "Hacia una definición" [Toward a definition]. Statement of the Chilean *Iglesia Joven* (Young Church) movement. Published in *NADOC,* no. 9 (Nov. 20, 1968). 14 pp

2. "El compromiso político de los cristianos" [Christian political involvement]. By the coordinating committee for the workshops on *la participación de los cristianos en la construcción del Socialismo* (Christian participation in the building of socialism). Intended as a "contribution" to the statement of the Chilean bishops. July 1971. Published in *Cristianos Latinoamericanos y Socialismo* [Latin American Christians and socialism] (Bogotá: CEDIAL, 1972), pp. 117–36.

3. "Comunidad de Cristianos Revolucionarios. Prima Declaración de principios" [Community of revolutionary Christians: First statement of principles]. Statement drawn up for a CfS community and published in Pablo Richard, *Cristianos por el Socialismo [CfS]: Historia y Documentación* [Christians for Socialism (CfS): History and documents] (Salamanco: Sígueme, 1976), pp. 239–41.

4. "Primer Encuentro Latinoamericano de Cristianos por el Socialismo" [First Latin American convention of Christians for Socialism]. Final document of the convention held at Santiago, Chile, April 23–30, 1972. In Alfredo Fierro and Reyes Mate, *Cristianos por el Socialismo* [Christians for socialism] (Estella, Navarre: Editorial Verbo Divino, 1975), pp. 283–302. Translated by John Drury in John Eagleson (ed.), *Christians and Socialism: Documentation of the Christians for Socialism Movement in Latin America* (Maryknoll, N.Y.: Orbis, 1975), pp. 160–75.

5. Conclusions of the commissions of the First Latin American Convention of Christians for Socialism (cf. no. 4, above), in *Los Cristianos y el Socialismo* [Christians and socialism] (Buenos Aires: Siglo Veintiuno, 1973).

Commission I. "Subdesarrollo, dependencia y transición al socialismo" [Underdevelopment, dependence, and transition to socialism], pp. 201–9.

Commission II. "Movilización popular" [Mobilization of the people], pp. 209–11.

Commission III. "Condiciones para una alianza estratégica entre cristianos y marzistas" [Conditions for a strategic alliance of Christians and Marxists], pp. 211–22.

Commission IV. "Ideología y religión: Revolución cultural y fe cristiana" [Ideology and religion: Cultural revolution and Christian faith], pp. 222–26.

Commission V. "Lucha de clases, posiciones y bloqueos éticos de los cristianos" [The class struggle: Christian positions and ethical barriers], pp. 226–31.

Commission VI. "Instituciones y ideologías cristianas" [Christian institutions and ideologies], pp. 231–36.

Commission VII. "Acción política y fe" [Political action and faith], pp. 236–40.

Commission VIII. "Partidos y sindicalismo del pueblo y práctica cristiana" [Popular parties, syndicalism, and Christian practice], pp. 240–44.

Commission IX. "Movimientos campesinos y acción de la Iglesias" [Rural movements and the action of the churches], pp. 245–48.

Commission X. "Capas medias y la mujer en la revolución" [Middle classes and women in the revolution], pp. 248–53.

6. "Del Social Cristianismo al Cristianismo Revolucionario" [From social Christianity to revolutionary Christianity]. Text of the Chilean report at the First Latin American Convention of CfS, 1972. Published in *Cristianos Latinoamericanos y Socialismo,* pp. 245–73, and translated in Eagleson, *Christians for Socialism* (*op. cit.,* no. 4, above), pp. 69–119.

7. Diego Irarrazával, "Cristianos en el proceso socialista" [Christians in the socialist process]. Paper read to National Chilean Workshop, November 25, 1972. Published in Fierro and Mate, *op. cit.,* pp. 413–86. The same text appears under the title "¿Qué hacer?" Richards (*op. cit.,* pp. 258–64) gives extracts from the text and says that it "is a theological, political, and programmatic document that accurately reflects the contents of the national meeting of November, 1972, and gives us a synthetic overview of the CfS movement at that stage of its existence. It is one of the most important basic documents of the Chilean CfS movement."

8. Gonzalo Arroyo S.J., "Significado y sentido de Cristianos por el Socialismo" ["Meaning and significance of CfS"]. An analysis of CfS in Chile, November 26, 1972. Published in Fierro and Mate, *op. cit.,* pp. 367–91.

9. "Lucha ideológica y nueva vivencia de la fe en los Cristianos por el Socialismo" [Ideological struggle and new experience of the faith among CfS]. Central section of the acts of the national CfS workshop, held at Santiago, Chile, November 24–26, 1972. Published in Fierro and Mate, *op. cit.,* pp. 253–68.

10. "Síntesis del trabajo de las comisiones y de la líneas centrales de la jornada nacional" [Synthesis of the work of the commissions and of the main lines of the national workshop (i.e., the workshop of Nov. 1972)]. Published in Richard, *op. cit.,* pp. 255–57.

11. "El Cristiano y la lucha de classes" [The Christian and the class struggle]. Position of the Christian Left in Chile, 1972. Published in Fierro and Mate, *op. cit.,* pp. 269–82.

12. "Cristianos por el Socialismo y las elecciones de marzo" [CfS and the March elections (in Chile, 1973)]. Partially published in Richard, *op. cit.*, pp. 152–54, 267–68.

13. "Definición Socialista de CpS" [Socialist definition of CfS]. A document of March 1973. Published in Richard, *op. cit.*, pp. 265–66.

14. "Resumen de los apuntes del encuentro de dirigentes de movimientos sacerdotales de América Latina" [Summary of the minutes of the meeting of leaders of the Latin American priests' movements]. The meeting was held in Lima, Peru, in 1973. On that occasion, the Latin American Federation of Priests' Movements was established. At that time the member groups were Priests for the Third World (Argentina), Priests for Socialism (Chile), National Independent Organization of Priests (Peru), Movement for Priestly Reflection (Ecuador), Priests for the People (Mexico), and Priests for Latin America (Colombia). Published in *Contacto* (Dec. 1973), pp. 75–80.

15. "Documento de Portugal" [The Portugal document]. Final statement of the National Meeting (Portugal) of CfS, January 1975. Published in Spanish in bulletin 4 (Jan.–Feb. 1975) of *Liaisons Internationales* (Paris), pp. 21–24.

16. "Documento de Avila" [The Avila document]. Composed in January 1973 and published in *Contacto,* no. 5 (Oct. 1973), pp. 80–88.

17. "Iniciación a la reflexión sobre fe cristiana y lucha de clases" [Introduction to reflection on Christian faith and the class struggle]. Catechetical material for discussion of disputed subjects. Appeared in Madrid toward the end of 1973. Published in Fierro and Mate, *op. cit.,* pp. 158–76.

18. "¿Qué es Cristianos por el Socialismo?" [What is CfS?]. Theoretical material compiled for the meeting that would discuss the March 1974 document (cf. next entry). Published in Fierro and Mate, *op. cit.*, pp. 177–93.

19. "Identidad y tareas de Cristianos por el Socialismo" [Iden-

tity and tasks of the CfS]. Extract from the March 1974 document, which relates to CfS in central Spain and is the end result of the meeting of the latter. Published in Fierro and Mate, *op. cit.,* pp. 194–200.

20. "Cristianos por el Socialismo en la emigración española" [CfS among emigrants from Spain]. In the spring of 1974 a meeting of Spanish emigrants was held to discuss CfS; about 100 people attended, coming from Germany, Switzerland, Holland, and France. The document is their final statement. Published in Fierro and Mate, *op. cit.,* pp. 201–21.

21. "Cristianos por el Socialismo: Un camino definitivamente abierto" [CfS: Commitment to a new direction]. Document drawn up by a group of 250 CfS at a meeting in Perpiñán, Spain, in 1974. Published in Fierro and Mate, *op. cit.,* pp. 222–36.

22. "Documento de Bolonia" [The Bologna document]. About 3,000 Italian Christians met at Bologna, September 21–31, 1973, to discuss the importance and timeliness of establishing CfS in Italy. The document is the result of the decision to go ahead. Published in Fierro and Mate, *op. cit.,* pp. 325–41.

23. "Documento de Nápoles" [The Naples document]. Statement of the second Italian meeting, April 1–4, 1974. Published in Spanish in Fierro and Mate, *op. cit.,* pp. 342–59.

24. "Documento de Québec" [The Quebec document]. The Second International Convention of CfS was held in Quebec in April 1975. This is the final statement. Published in *Medellín* (1976), pp. 144–50.

25. "Caminos de una nueva vivencia de la fe" [Ways to a new experience of the faith]. Document of the First Commission of the Second International Convention of CfS, Quebec, April 1975. Reprinted in bulletin 11 of the SAL group of Medellín, pp. 7–13.

26. "Los Cristianos por el Socialismo y la Iglesia" [CfS and the Church]. Document of the Second Commission of the Second International Convention of CfS, Quebec, April 1975. Reprinted in bulletin 12 of the SAL group of Medellín, pp. 3–7.

27. "Los Cristianos por el Socialismo y la lucha política" [CfS and the political struggle]. Document of the Third Commission of the Second International Convention of CfS, Quebec, April 1975. Reprinted in bulletin 12 of the SAL group of Medellín, pp. 8–10.

28. "Aspectos del desarrollo de caitalismo mundial y de la coyuntura actual" [Aspects of the development of world capitalism and of the present conjuncture]. Document of the Fourth Commission of the Second International Convention of CfS, Quebec, April 1975. Reprinted in bulletin 13 of the SAL group of Medellín, pp. 3–15, and bulletin 14, pp. 3–9.

29. "Definición sintética de Cristianos por el Socialismo" [Synthetic definition of CfS]. Document of the Fifth Commission of the Second International Convention of CfS, Quebec, April 1975. Reprinted in bulletin 14 of the SAL group of Medellín, pp. 9–12.

30. "Documento final" [Final statement]. Document of the Second National Congress of the National (Ecuadorian) Movement of Christians for Liberation. Published in bulletin 18 (May 1975) of the movement, pp. 6–10.

31. "Cristianos por el Socialismo de Puerto Rico" [CfS in Puerto Rico]. Document of November 1975. Published in *Liaisons Internationales*. bulletin 9 (April–June 1976), pp. 32–39.

32. "Notas de una Iglesia Popular" [Marks of a Church of the People]. Document from the April 1974 meeting of the Faith Integrated with Action Movement (Peru). Published in *Liaisons Internationales,* bulletin 4 (Jan.–Feb. 1975), pp. 11–12.

33. "Documento de trabajo que intenta una expresión de lo que es la Iglesia Solidaria" [Working paper aimed at a statement of what the "Integral Church" is]. Mexico, 1975. Published in *Liaisons Internationales,* bulletin 7 (Sept.–Nov. 1975), pp. 32–35.

34. Workshop on "Reinterpretation of the Faith," held in Spain, 1976. Reflected in a CfS document published in *Pastoral Popular,* no. 146 (Oct.–Dec. 1976), pp. 20–30.

1. The "Church of the People," according to Christians for Socialism (CfS)

This is not the place for sketching the history of CfS[3] or for offering a bibliography on the movement.[4] It is enough to point out that there have thus far been two key moments in the development of the movement: the First Latin American Convention of CfS, held at Santiago, Chile, April 23–30, 1972, and the International Convention, held at Quebec in April 1975 (also called the Second Convention).

Latin America

The term "Church of the People" does not occur in the final document of the First Latin American Convention of CfS. The idea expressed in the name is indeed present, however, in the criticism of the "institutional Church" (4/I, 1, 6), in the rejection of the Church's social teaching as "reformism" (I, 1, 13) and a fruitless "third way" (I, 1, 16), in the "growing awareness that revolutionary Christians must form a strategic alliance with Marxists within the liberation process on this continent" (I, 3, 7), in the assertion that socialism is the only possible alternative to dependent capitalism (I, 1, 13; II, 1, 3), in the judgment that the ideological struggle is "an essential component" of revolutionary action (II, 2, 2), in the rejection of the distinctively Christian contribution "to the appearance of the New Man" (II, 3, 2), in the discovery that "a love which brings about transformation is lived out in antagonism and confrontation" and that "the unity of the Church comes about through the unity of humanity" (II, 3, 6), and in the felt need of "a new reading of the Bible and of Christian tradition" and of recasting "the basic concepts and symbols of Christianity . . . in such a way that they do not hamper Christians in their commitment to the revolutionary process" (II, 3, 8).

The ten commissions set up at the convention in Chile used stronger language than did the final official statement.

Commission I claims that "we may generalize for all of Latin America and say whenever a Christian or group of Christians become effectively involved with their fellows who are suffering from underdevelopment and exploitation, conflict with the institutional Church is inevitable" (5/no. 5), and that as a result "they are shunted aside by their Churches." This leads them to look for "another Church." The commission goes on to say: "A revolutionary conception of the class struggle within the Church shows us that the Church must undergo a conversion in its methods if the faith itself is to be liberated. The revolution is the way to a new Church" (no. 6). The commission is therefore convinced that "a break with and a struggle against the institutional Church will be the best path for the revolution to take." According to the commission, "the Church is a superstructure. Its message is an ideology which the ruling classes and the rich countries have made use of down to the present time."

Commission III, which deals with "conditions for a strategic alliance of Christians and Marxists," concludes that "it is impossible to form a strategic alliance if we employ the forces of traditional, institutional Christianity" (1,1). Consequently, it is Christianity, not Marxism, that must be changed. "There are Christians who realize that the faith is neither a religion nor an ideology and that they do not have a political method specific to them as Christians. They struggle alongside the Marxists and discover that historical materialism (which provides them with an analysis and method of action) is complementary to faith in Jesus Christ the Liberator. Without historical materialism they must persist in attitudes that are characteristic of reformist Christianity and an obstacle to an authentic revolution" (2.3).

The same commission urges the authentic Christian to a "revolutionary involvement" as the "basis for any contribution Christians can make" (4.1). "Involvement" or "commitment" means "to choose the side of all the oppressed and to share their struggle for freedom from exploitation" (ibid.) so as to "attain the power contained in the dictatorship of the proletariat" (cf. 3.2). For this reason, the commission "urges that Christian circles be introduced to the scientific analysis of reality, and urges participation in organizations of the people so as to advance the revolutionary process. This task must be carried on in the light of a correct study of strategy" (4.3). The commission likewise urges Christians "to live by, and communicate, the revolutionary faith as contrasted with a reactionary or reformist type of Christianity, by creating new forms wherein the faith may find expression" (4.4). This participation in the struggle of the people "brings with it the conquest of bourgeois moralism and the power to use revolutionary means, which cannot be understood apart from the process" (4.5).

It is likewise necessary to affirm "the primacy of revolutionary action" (5.2). "By adopting this primacy, Christians transform their bourgeois Christianity into a liberating faith, and accept the autonomy of science and revolutionary action. In this sense they must purify the faith. The building of a socialist society is a nonreligious task and presupposes a religionless Christianity" (ibid.).

This whole process of change naturally raises problems as to membership in the Church. "Generally speaking, revolutionary Christians either leave or are excluded from the Church as an institution. Some set aside traditional practices to devote themselves entirely to liberation. Others form leftist cells or communities, wherein they find a renewed faith. If their faith does not find expression in new forms, they will retain reactionary commitments that are an obstacle to the process of liberation. For this reason, it is necessary to declericalize Christianity, to democratize it, and to restore to it its revolutionary impulse" (5.4). This is the "new Christianity" that is the indispensable foundation of the "Church of the People."

For Commission IV, the "important thing, as the parable of the last judgment (Matthew 25) shows, is not to know oneself to be a Christian but to liberate those who are oppressed."

Commission VII, which dealt with "political action and faith," likewise calls for new ways of living the faith. "There is no hope that such new forms will arise within the bosom of the Church.

It is only the revolutionary process itself that can lead to a revolution within the Church. The Church must be willing to be continually challenged, for the Church is in fact an obstacle that prevents many Christians from being truly involved in liberation. Today, more than in other times, the Church must be made over and renewed" (5/pp. 239–40).

Commission VIII thinks there is an unavoidable danger that committed Christians will in fact abandon their traditional faith. But, according to the commission, "pratcice of the faith is implicit in revolutionary practice. A person is more of a Christian the more he or she shares in the struggles of the people for their liberation" (5/p. 244).

Such were the views of 170 Catholic priests, 30 religious women, 160 lay people, and 40 members of various Christian denominations when they gathered in April 1972 for the First CfS Convention. We shall not embark at this point on a critico-theological analysis of their statements, but it is not difficult to see the kind of new church — the "Church of the People" — that would arise if all the foregoing assertions were taken seriously. When confronted with such statements and their astounding theological superficiality, one spontaneously asks: Would such a "Church of the People" still be our one, holy, and catholic Church?

A few months later, in November 1972, a National Workshop of the Chilean CfS was held. On this occasion, Gonzalo Arroyo S.J., secretary general of the CfS, said: "We look forward to a new Church that will not be under the thumb of the institution, for the law of self-preservation governs all that the institution does. Its ways are heavy and harsh, and the structures now existing in the Church seek to protect and preserve themselves. Getting rid of them will be costly. Our new Church, which we yearn for and aspire to, is a Church proper to a world already secularized" (8/p. 385).

"We must build a Church especially of the poor, a Church that has nothing to do with the mighty, a Church that draws its nourishment exclusively from its base, has a minimum of the institutional about it, and is committed to the liberation of human beings" (p. 386). This eagerness for a "new Church" also appears on other pages of this paper: "We seek a new Church" (p. 388); "We look forward to this new Church in which all will be included, evangelicals as well as Catholics" (pp. 389–90).

The secretary general of CfS proposes a whole program:

> We have not devoted enough effort to seeking new ways of living our faith and celebrating the Eucharist, to finding a whole new way of administering the sacraments (the present one is often colored by the dominant ideology), to developing a new spirituality and new forms of prayer. None of these have been developed as yet. We have only just begun. A new and necessary field of action lies before us — more necessary than ever in a process like ours which makes so many demands on us and requires so much sacrifice. We see how people exhaust themselves, how those committed to the cause are spendthrift with their energies and need to have in their community the additional power of the Spirit; they need a kind of surplus value that is spiritual, not economic, and comes precisely from the Christian community. We have not done enough work in this area. It is an area in which we must advance [p. 380].

At the same workshop, Diego Irarrazával spoke as follows:

> The most important thing is that we have been revising our relationship with the entire ecclesial institution. As Christians of the left, situated now on the side of the oppressed and struggling people, we stand in a new relation to the rest of the Church. We realize that to live, as we have hitherto, in a direct confrontation of Christian base with hierarchy, is to accept the rules of the game that have been established by the reactionaries. Why have we been changing all this? Because the important thing is the integration of Christians with the people in their quest of liberation. It is on that basis, that is, on the basis of the struggle of the poor for liberation,

> that we live and work within the institutional Church. This mediating link is very important because it provides a new framework for our relations with pastors, bishops, leaders generally, and pastoral organizations. Amid our communion with the oppressed and their struggle a new ecclesial communion is coming to birth [7/pp. 457–58].

In all this the expression "Church of the People" does not appear. But we do have here the ideological context of popular struggle in which will arise the desire for a "Church of the People" and for all the changes in faith and action that its ideologists will demand.

Irarrazával continues: "We have found that Christians cannot be committed to the revolution unless their faith is radically changed" (pp. 469–70). "I honestly believe that all of us gathered here have been converted, or that we have recently had a new experience of conversion. It is not just certain of our political commitments or ideological positions that have changed. Our faith itself has changed" (p. 476).

Again: "Thus, the whole expression of our faith has changed. In order to take their place at the heart of history, the symbols of faith have become historical and an embodiment of the hope for liberation. In prayer, in understanding of the Gospel message, in sacraments and Eucharist: in all these we have made a qualitative leap" (p. 477).

These programmatic texts of 1972 will be repeated later at the many other CfS meetings and in related movements. It is clear that the "newness" being sought and, above all, the "qualitative leap" proclaimed in these texts must have a radical effect on theology, and especially on the "new" kind of faith and, consequently, on the treatise that deals with the Church — (unless, of course, we are content simply to renounce entirely the traditional faith and theology).

Internationally

Three years later, at its meeting in Quebec in April 1975, the CfS was able to verify the claim that "the stream of Christians committed to struggles for liberation has broadened and become stronger throughout the world."[5] The final, official statement of the Quebec convention shows that those who attended it had reflected "on the rise of a Christianity that is proletarian and popular in nature and capable of emancipating itself from the dominant bourgeois ideology" (24/no. 2).

At Quebec, the CfS members may almost be said to have defined themselves in terms of their decision to create this "new Church":

> A growing number of Christians in all five continents are joining in the struggles for popular liberation. These Christians make up a large body that is defined by a new quest for faith and for new ecclesial forms, within a political practice that is proletarian and socialist in character. Though involved in and, in a sense, dispersed in the political struggle, they nonetheless unite in carrying on within Christianity an ideological struggle whose importance seems to be constantly increasing. This action provides new motives for gathering into committed Christian communities that are evolving a type of evangelization which aims at liberation and at sowing the seeds of a Church of the People. There is thus arising a Christianity that is linked to the interests of the working class and provides an alternative to a Christianity that is allied, ideologically and structurally, to the dominant exploitative system [24/no. 28].

The same document devotes nos. 15–19 to a "new practice of the faith" and nos. 20–28 to "new forms of ecclesial life." Although the CfS members do not feel at home in the Church, "they refuse nonetheless to depart from the Churches and leave the Gospel in the possession of the ruling classes. It is this opposition and the suffering it has caused that have led to the search for an ecclesial alternative" (no. 24)

The search for an ecclesial alternative emerges more clearly in the documents of the five commissions set up at the convention. The First Commission, which dealt with "ways to a new experience of the faith," takes up "the subversive practice of the poor," that is, "poor" in the sense of "oppressed." To take the side of these poor means a break with a "bourgeois," individualistic kind of Christian life and with the "ideologization" of the faith that has been effected by the ruling classes (25/1.2).

The commission insists, however, that "the poor must liberate themselves; they must be the agents of their own emancipation" (2.2), and they alone (2.4). "The poor are the builders both of history and of the Church" (2.7). "That is why we break with the manipulative practice of going out and evangelizing the people as though we were the owners of the truth. The people is evangelized when it begins to evangelize itself."

This is a central idea of the commission, and one it regards as extremely important. Such an idea represents a radical change in the very concept of evangelization and of the mission Christ gave to his apostles. The "conversion" sought is a "conversion to the people" (3.1). This strange notion of conversion comes up frequently in the various documents.[6]

This first document emphasizes "the salvific value of political commitment" (3.5). "We see in the practice of liberation a communion with Christ in the oppressed and an approach of the kingdom. This is fundamental and the abiding condition for strengthening the Church and for promoting the evangelization that is carried on by the poor. But we now have a better grasp of the ecclesial and evangelizing value of practice. We are concerned with using political practice to create the conditions needed for the Church of the poor to come into existence." Nevertheless, "if the poor do not become the agents who transform history, political practice has no value for evangelization."

The commission also asserts this further principle: "We affirm the right and power of the poor to interpret and put into practice the liberating word. The Gospel clearly suggests this, for Jesus tells us that the humble, the poor, and the oppressed are the ones who hear his message and put it into practice" (4.2).

This commission also calls for "the social appropriation of the Gospel." "The poor have the sensitivity and capacity for accepting the word of the Lord and putting it into practice as a people" (4.6). Other men and women read the Bible as individualists; the "poor" appropriate the word in a "social" way.

The Second Commission, which took for its subject "Christians for Socialism and the Church," states that "it has already been proved beyond doubt that as it lives in the world the Church forms a conception of Christianity and a plan for society that are identical with those of capitalist society" (26/1.2), and that the ecclesial institution has been "taken over by the ruling powers and used as an ideological tool for perpetuating the status quo" (2.0).

All of this necessitates a renewal of the Church. To this end, the commission proposes "an alternative kind of ecclesial life that is based on a revolutionary practice" (no. 2). The latter includes a choice of a particular class (2.1) and the formation of a "Church of the People" (2.2) "in which the Gospel is given back to the poor and in which the message, coming from the poor, regains its full power, having been liberated from wrongful appropriation by the bourgeoisie." It will be accompanied by "new expressions of faith" (2.4), a new liturgy (ibid.), a rereading of the Bible (2.5), and a ministry of the people (2.6). In this new "Church of the People," in which "a class practice provides the framework," the people are acknowledged to be "the critical court of appeal. There will be "a new prophetic ministry exercised by the people," a "new leadership that does not regard itself as repository of the truth," a "new *diaconia* or service," and a "new interpretation of ministry and charism that sees a positive connection between the two" (2.6).

Such is the new "alternative form of ecclesial life" (no. 3).

Christians for Socialism, however, seeks to live this alternative form within the institutional Church.

> We do not as yet have any experience of this new reality. The ecclesial life now dominant always transmits an ideological Gospel and a depoliticized practice. If we are to achieve our own liberation, we must resist that kind of transmission, and we hope to do so within the Churches themselves. Both the revolutionary struggle and the faith itself require this of us. We can no longer tolerate such an ideologization of Christian life. Our faith in Jesus Christ as risen and alive today rouses us to put his liberating power to work. Our revolutionary struggle forbids us to leave the Churches. To leave the Churches would be to hand over to the ruling classes both the Gospel and the Spirit who makes the Gospel give life [III.2.1].

The reasons for not leaving the churches are really tactical, but the commission realizes it would be more logical simply to leave. The commission then proposes the following "strategic moves."

1. Strengthening the roots of the CfS in the struggle of the people and in the community formed by the people. The struggle that is carried on by the people "is decisive for our reading of the Gospel, our relation to Jesus Christ, and our life in the Church. . . . The vitality of Christian communities involved in the people's struggle is what will, in the last analysis, enable us to effect a total change in the Church."

2. Promoting pluralism. "Our struggle within the Church begins and continues in a liberal context characterized by pluralism." The development of an alternative Church life is favored by the present pluralist conjuncture. The commission warns, however, that this alternative Church life, which is tolerated in the contemporary pluralist atmosphere, must not be relativized as one option alongside others: "Our class option is not a relative option, but is clearly demanded by the revolutionary struggle that will bring about a socialist society in which all social relations are

radically transformed" and in which neither pluralism nor the possibility of any other option will be admissible.

3. Challenging the progressives. There are groups which fail to understand the mechanisms that give structure to capitalist society, which contaminate the Church's life, and which kill the prophetic impulse in the Church. "Our task is to work with these groups and enable them to attain to a scientific analysis of society and thus to become part of the revolutionary struggle."[7]

The Third Commission, on "Christians for Socialism and the political struggle," establishes that the specific function of CfS in the workers' movement is "an ideological struggle to stir Christians to make a political choice among the Marxist revolutionary parties" (27/1.1). Christians are to be moved by "bringing home to them the revolutionary demands faith makes, among which are included, in our day, the building of a socialist society."

Christians must also be shown "alternative expressions of the faith" (cf. the Second Commission's "alternative form of ecclesial life"), but "a primary purpose of this ideological work must be the development of the class struggle within the institutional Church. This will break down the monolithic uniformity that generally characterizes the Church (1.3).

The commission also claims that "there is a genuine unity among Marxists, Christians, and atheists" (3.4).

The Fourth Commission, on "aspects of the development of world capitalism and of the present conjuncture," repeats some of the same ideas. Thus it states that the specific role of CfS in the workers' movement is

> an ideological struggle to stir Christians to make a political choice among the revolutionary or Marxist parties. This involves showing them the revolutionary demands the faith makes, and the harmony between the faith and Marixst socialism. . . . The outcome must

> be a strategic revolutionary alliance between Christians and atheistic Marxists [28/no. 1].

It is likewise "the responsibility of CfS to show alternative expressions of the faith at the level of the working class. This will enable the militants from the revolutionary organizations to challenge the conservative ways of expressing the faith that still persist." In addition, "it is necessary to bring to light possible tactical alliances between the revolutionary forces and tendencies, movements, or persons within the Churches." These remarks occur in no. 1 of part III, which has the title "Role of Christians for Socialism."

In no. 5, under the title "CfS and Christian Social 'Third Way' Views," we read:

> The chief responsibility of CfS when confronted with these institutions [i.e., Christian social institutions such as trade unions, worker movements, rural movements, apostolic movements, etc.] is to denounce the ideologization of the faith such movements represent, their political inadequacy, and their supposed manifestation of the Christian conscience as such. Especially to be denounced is "Christian social teaching" as being a way by which the ruling class maintains its power.

The Fifth Commission, which worked on a "synthetic definition of CfS," says that one of the "common grounds" uniting different yet similar movements is "the aim of breaking up the ideological freeze in which Christians find themselves, and thus making it possible for them to share the revolutionary militancy of the people" (29/1.3).

No. 4 contains a very important statement:

> The confrontations between our movements and the ecclesiastical authorities must be seen in the wider perspective of our responsibility in the struggle of the people. In this area, the chief aim, with few exceptions, must be not to let ourselves be isolated within the

> Churches, while at the same time not letting ourselves become the tool, within the Churches or outside of them, of a procapitalist and interclassist orientation.

We must pay careful attention to two pieces of advice given in this text, for they explain the behavior of not a few clerics and religious in recent years:

1. "Not to let ourselves be isolated" and, therefore, to be "present" and thus able to promote the ideological struggle within the Church. No. 7 deals with the ideological struggle and the specific practice that must be followed "in the bosom of the Churches."

2. "Not to let ourselves become a tool" explains the steady unwillingness of CfS to engage in authentic dialogue. The members do not enter into dialogue (and thus they say they are incorruptible), but they demand that *others* engage in dialogue so that they (CfS) can speak out and begin their ideological struggle. They themselves are not pluralists (their choice is absolute), but they demand that others manifest a pluralism that is unlimited.

To give ourselves a concrete idea of what, in the CfS view, a community of the "Church of the People" would be like, we may take as an example the community of Forestal Alto, Viña del Mar, Chile. This community drew up the following "initial statement of principles."[8]

> 1. Camillo Torres and Che Guevara said: "Every Christian has a duty to be a revolutionary, and every revolutionary has a duty to effect the revolution." It is in the light of these words that a Community of Revolutionary Christians is hereby established at Forestal Alto, Viña del Mar, Chile, on Sunday, October 17, 1971. The objective of the community is to live its faith in Christ within the Chilean revolution.
>
> 2. Two conditions are required for membership in this community: to be a Christian and to be a revolutionary, or at least to be open to being both.

3. Unlike other Christian communities, this one exercises a discrimination; no one can be a member unless first accepted by the existing members.

4. On this condition, however, the community is open to everyone and seeks to play a decisive part in the reform of the entire Church, so that the true Church of the future, that is, a Church of revolutionaries, may be formed.

5. In order that the Church may not detract in the slightest from the revolutionary commitment of its members, it must meet according to a rhythm that will not lessen that commitment. Ordinarily, then, there shall be a monthly gathering in the evening of the first Sunday of each month; this does not prevent the holding of extraordinary meetings at the request of the community or the committee in authority.

6. The following elements are to be included in one or another way in the community gathering: review of the revolutionary commitment, agape or fraternal meal, commentary on the Gospel, Eucharist.

7. The members of the community promise to give first priority to the monthly meeting, in which they give expression to their faith in the unqualified primacy of God's reign that comes through every revolutionary act. If an individual cannot be faithful to this promise, some member of the committee in authority must be told in advance. The committee will act as a revolutionary tribunal, and the member may be expelled from the community.

8. To finance the life of the community (fraternal meal; educational material; etc.), each member must contribute 1% of his net monthly income.

9. Individuals must reapply each month for membership in the community. This implies that no one has a right to membership unless he is a Christian and an active revolutionary.

10. Although the community is located at Forestal Alto, people from other geographical areas can be members. This policy is adopted because nowadays there are many revolutionary Christians who are forced to live their faith in isolation, inasmuch as they have no access to Churches that express all their concerns.

11. The acceptance of these principles is a strict obligation on all members of the community. Only a revolutionary discipline can

lead us to revolutionary moral conduct. Only a revolutionary moral conduct can lead us to a revolutionary Christianity. Only a revolutionary Christianity can help liberate man.

2. The "Church of the People," according to Related Movements

At the International Convention in Quebec, Commission V stated that "CfS takes various forms and even various names. In any case, what gives coherence to the movement is not the name but the struggle and a practice of the faith that is consistent with the struggle and with certain clear and precisely defined goals" (29/no. 13).

As a matter of fact, "informal" groups are arising everywhere — "liberated" communities, "prophetic" movements, "committed" priests, Christians "in solidarity," "searching" Christians, or simply groups "for reflection." In Colombia, for example, in addition to the CfS are Priests for Latin America (SAL),[9] Organization of Priest Workers at the Base Level (OSTB), Intercultural Committee for Dialogue and Action in Latin America (CIDALA), Latin American Institute for Pastoral Action among the People (ILAPP), Religious Women for a New Church, Organization of Religious Women for Latin America (ORAL), Priests for the Poor, Committee of Priests and Religious Women for the Defense of Human Rights, Christians for Liberation. The Colombian Social Communications Service (SCCS) provides these groups with a vehicle for information and agitation.

Let us look more closely at a few of these movements.

I. At Lima, in February 1973, various movements of priests formed a federation with Gustavo Gutiérrez as its president.[10] The groups were Priests for the Third World (Argentina), Priests for

Socialism (Chile), National Independent Organization of Priests (ONIS) (Peru), Movement for Priestly Reflection (Ecuador), Priests for the People (Mexico), and Priests for Latin America (Colombia).

In essence, a "Summary of the Minutes" for this meeting[11] repeats the principles of the CfS. Here again, "it is the popular classes and especially the proletariat that are to bring about the radical transformation of the present social order" (14/1.A.1). Here again, "men of faith who make their own the yearnings and struggles of the oppressed classes feel the tension between the ideologized bourgeois faith which they have inherited and which characterizes our society, and the more authentic faith which is discovered when they take a faithful part in the revolutionary political process" (ibid.). Here again, "the Christian must, above all else, take part in revolutionary practice, identify with the concerns of the proletariat, make them his own, and share in the struggles and yearnings of the people" (1.A.2). Here again, such an approach and behavior will "transform our way of living and thinking the faith" (ibid.). Here again, Christians are to "choose socialism" (1.C). Here again, the aim is "a rereading of the faith" (2.B) and a "Church of the People" (2.C).

Concerning this so-called Church, the leaders of the Latin American Priests' Movements state:

> [1.] The new Church that we desire must begin now to develop. This development requires concrete anticipatory gestures in the form of actions by an ecclesial community that has participation in the proletarian struggle as its foundation.
>
> [2.] In this way we seek to share in the building of the Church of the future. The aim is not to create another Church or a counter-Church, but to build a new Church in which the proletariat, the social class today oppressed and marginalized, can have its own voice. Evangelization must foster a people whose faith will project its own Church.
>
> [3.] In building this Church of the future, we must, as we pointed out above, have before our minds the fact that the political

> dimension is at the very heart of the Gospel, as it is of all historical reality. It follows that the entire work of evangelization necessarily has a politicizing function; in a society like ours, this means accepting the fact of the class struggle and taking sides unambiguously with the exploited classes.

It is not difficult to see that the "Church of the People" that is proper to these movements of priests in Latin America is closely related to the "Church of the People" of which CfS speaks. The terminology, goals, and underlying ideology are more or less the same. Later, we will see that methods, tactics, and strategies are also the same. Here we wish to emphasize the aim of sharing in the "proletarian struggle," accepting the "fact" of the class struggle, and taking the side of the "exploited" classes. The "Church of the People," which will be the much desired "new Church," or even the "Church of the future," will be an essentially politicized church to which only the proletariat will belong. No one else will have voice or vote in it.

In the final part of the document, the leaders of the priests' movements set their priorities as far as immediate tasks are concerned. "Ours will be the important task of contributing to the advancement of a Church that is committed to the oppressed and to the exploited classes. This will lead to a rereading of our faith." A new faith.

II. In April 1974 there was a meeting of the leaders of the popular groups that make up the Movement for Solidarity in Faith and Action (Peru). The purpose of the meeting was to gain a deeper understanding of their ecclesial option and to sketch a clearer picture of the kind of church the movement should seek to develop so that the community might play a greater part in the history of the country. According to the document "Marks of a Church of the People" (32), which resulted from this meeting,[12] the marks of an "authentically popular" church are

1. A classist church; that is, the ecclesial community must de-

fine itself in terms of a clear identification with the concerns of the people. It must put itself forthrightly at the service of the people.

2. A church that is poor and of the poor, in which the popular classes have voice and vote. This church must be "inhospitable to the privileged and the powerful. It will evidently not exclude people who come from classes other than the people, but it will require of them a specific class option." The more fully aware sectors of the popular classes will be the ones who "will express the faith and determine the life of the ecclesial community."
3. A church which protests against every injustice. This requires "a special concern for sin within the Church."
4. A church that transforms man. But "the transformation in question is not individualistic, in the sense that the person is converted to something more 'correct' or more 'pious.' The person's correctness and piety, his real transformation, will be shown by a change in his way of life, by a love that commits him more fully each day to the popular classes and makes him more involved in their transformation."
5. A church that proclaims, lives, and celebrates the liberating message of the Gospel, but always "within the class option."

III. The "Final Statement" of the Second National Congress of the National Movement of Christians for Liberation (MNCL), held at Riobamba, Ecuador, in 1975 (which is led by Catholic priests), takes the same line and shows similar emphases. According to this group, the Second Vatican Council "disowned forever any ecclesial monolithicism, took an undogmatic approach to the theoretical treatment of human and social problems, and introduced pluralism into theology" (30/1.1). They believe, therefore, that they have been given a green light for developing a new ecclesiology that will be based on the "theology of liberation" (1.4). They maintain that "the communion of men with one another and with the Father can come to pass only through the creation of a new man (who is neither exploiter nor exploited) in a new society (which, in the conjuncture, is a socialist society). This is possible, in turn, only if the proletariat seizes political power; in other words, only if there is a dictatorship of the proletariat, for this must be the form a genuine popular democracy takes" (2.2). This group asserts, in addition, "the necessity of using the tools provided by Marxist analysis" (ibid.), and it therefore aims "at the establishment of a Church of the People."

The more specific proposals of the congress (in no. 4 of the document) are

1. To keep up the ideological struggle with the hierarchy;
2. To defeat the anti-Marxist, anti-Communist, and antirevolutionary position;
3. To reject any position that opts for a "third way" and focuses on "community," such as "the only Catholic way" of the Cardinal of Quito. "We point out, however, that while practical plans for community may have no strategic value, they may nonetheless serve, in a particular situation, as a tactical means of strengthening the power of the people";
4. To reject the reactionary outlook of such groups as the Pentecostals, the "Communal Creativity" group, etc.;
5. To reject uncompromisingly the positions of such groups as Opus Dei, etc.;
6. To develop a more profound theology of "liberation," so as to provide more solid foundations for faith and revolutionary commitment;
7. To foster the development of the "Church of the People," in which the living of the Gospel is intimately linked with concrete historical struggles;
8. To maintain solidarity with all those bishops (Bishop Proaño, e.g.) who are working for the establishment of a "Church of the People" which will be involved in the popular struggle for "liberation."

This Second National Congress received a telegram of

support from Bishop Méndez Arceo of Cuernavaca (Mexico), addressed to Bishop Leonidas Proaño of Riobamba: "Convey my hopes, my sense of solidarity and fellowship, to the Christians for Liberation at their meeting." Thus the group did not lack the support of some bishops.

IV. In 1975, somewhere in Mexico (the exact place and date are not known), a group of "farmers, masons, religious women, teachers, unmarried mothers, woodcutters, and workers young and old, male and female," met and drew up a "Working Paper Aimed at a Statement of What the 'Integral Church' Is" (document no. 33).[13] The idiom of the statement is that of the people, but the statement is surprisingly exact in its formulation of concepts. (We have met the concepts in previous documents.)

This group repeats the same harsh accusations against the Church: "In the Church, too, the bosses give the orders; we poor people must simply listen as we are told that our part is to be resigned, to obey, and to take part in worship and in the feasts of the saints." They have heard nothing but that — even after the Second Vatican Council and the teaching of the Latin American bishops at Medellín!

"Priests and especially the bishops gave their blessing and support in the old days to the property owners and the bosses; today they give it to the bankers and the industrialists."

"For many years they taught us to pray a lot, to attend solemn Masses for the dead and, in general, to make the dead the center of our religion." As if the Church has never been interested in the living.

In addition, the powerful of this world "have taught us to harass our brothers" and have convinced us "that if we do not abandon others, we will never get anywhere." Now they find that they are fed up with "a Church that buys and sells, that requires an obedience inspired by fear, that looks for resignation and talks about saving souls, but is not on our side."

This is why Christians are now looking for a different kind of church.

> As we struggle, we seek to establish a new Church that corresponds to what Christ wants: a Church in which we have the right to speak, a Church in which we celebrate the progress of the struggle which we are carrying on in fellowship with those who do not have the faith but who are likewise battling against the enemies of the people. In striving for this goal, we are aware that in the statements of the bishops, in the rituals and songs of our Church, in the way in which Christian life is presented to us, and in the decisions made, our Church sees through the eyes of the rich, speaks with the deceitful tongue of those who oppress us, and in her action uses the symbols and expresses the views of the powerful.

Moreover:

> Amid the struggle we are endeavoring to build a Church of the People in which preaching, decisions, symbols, and institutions will be consistent with the ideals for which our fathers and grandfathers fought, for which we are fighting now, and for which we want our sons to fight. We wish to follow Christ as poor men from all the little corners of the land, men brought together by Christ in order to establish a new Church in a new society. We are working for an integral Church that gathers in all the poor.

V. Thus far we have been examining only representative documents issued by groups. Now we turn to statements by individuals, such as Hugo Assmann in "Iglesia Popular" [Church of the People], *Contacto* (Dec. 1975), pp. 22–29; Francisco Vanderhoff and Miguel Angel Campos in "La Iglesia Popular: Condiciones político-ideológicas para su surgimiento" [Political and ideological conditions for the establishment of a Church of the People], *Contacto* (Dec. 1975); Raúl Vidales in "Evangelización y liberación popular" [Evangelization and the liberation of the people], in *Liberación y cautiverio* (papers of the Latin American Congress of Theology) (Mexico City, 1975), especially pp. 221–26; Gustavo Gutiérrez in "Revelación y anuncio de Dios en la historia" [Revelation and the proclamation of God in history], *Pastoral Popular,* no. 146 (Oct.–Dec. 1976), especially pp. 41–42. As a matter of fact, all these writers are saying more or less the same thing, as we shall now see.

For Hugo Assmann, the important thing is to "lay the foundations for a new Church that will fight for the liberation of the oppressed" (p. 24).

According to Francisco Vanderhoff and Miguel Angel Campos, we must create the conditions for the kind of change in ecclesiastical structures that will enable the thirst for liberation to find expression "in the concrete form of a Church of the People" (p. 56). "We believe that such conditions can only be created outside the present structures of the Church, in an 'exodus' into the world of the oppressed, for that is the only world in which a Church of the People is now taking shape and can possibly take shape" (ibid.).

According to Gustavo Gutiérrez, "when the Gospel is read from the viewpoint of the poor, the exploited classes, and those struggling for liberation, it cries out for a Church of the People. This means a Church born of the people, that is, a people that wrests the Gospel from the hands of the powerful and prevents its being used as justification for a situation that is contrary to the will of the God who sets men free" (pp. 41–42). According to Gutiérrez, the poor (who alone are the "people") must effect a "social appropriation of the Gospel," taking it away from those who look upon it as their private possession. "Evangelization will become a truly liberating process when the poor themselves do the evangelizing."

Nowadays, ever since Vatican II, says Gutiérrez, "we understand better that we are called to build the Church from below, that is, in terms of the poor, the exploited classes, the marginalized races, and the cultures that men scorn. That is what it means to build a Church of the People."

Raúl Vidales acknowledges that "a Church of the People will inevitably be subversive and dangerous to the established order both civil and religious" (p. 224). In his view, "once classist Christian communities have concrete experience of the Gospel in their advance toward liberation, the new face of a 'new people' and therefore of a new *Church* will gradually reveal its features. This will not be a Church that resignedly submits, but a Church that arises out of an historical context of struggle, repression, clandestinity, and captivity" (ibid.). The issue, he says, is "to create a new *Church* by liberating the oppressed."

A Note on the Brazilian "Church Born of the People"

In January 1975 and July 1976 the First and Second National Congresses of Base Communities were held at Vitória, capital of the state of Espíritu Santo. At these two congresses the central theme was "the Church that is born of the people." The documents produced by the first congress were published in *SEDOC* (May 1975), pp. 1061–1216; the documents of the second in *SEDOC* (Oct. 1976), pp. 259–448 and (Nov. 1976) 449–575.

The short final document of the second congress speaks four times of "the Church that is born of the people," which is ambiguous. Theologically speaking, it must be said that "it was from the side of Christ as He slept the sleep of death upon the cross that there came forth the wondrous sacrament which is the whole Church" (*SC,* 5b/140). Or, as the Council teaches in its Dogmatic Constitution on the Church, the inauguration and growth of the Church are symbolized by the blood and water which flowed from the open side of the crucified Christ (*LG,* 3b/16). Consequently, "the Church that is born of the people" is simply a rhetorical figure and says no more than that, here and now, the Church in a given place, with its particular situations and problems, must be so present, or incarnated, that it is identified as far as possible with the people for whom it exists and in function of whom it operates. This means that the people (i.e., all the baptized, not only the poor) are to participate actively, as far as the condition, vocation, and charism of each individual allow, in the mission of the Church. In this sense, the Church is and must be very much a "popular" Church or a Church "of and for the people."

In the Brazilian statements, "people" seems to be equivalent to "the very poor." But this is because the ecclesial base communities are set up chiefly among the most deprived people in the rural areas (in Brazil, the rural areas are frequently very poor even today) or in the poor quarters of the major cities. A legitimate, necessary, and laudable preference is to be given to the poor, as the Gospel itself commands, but preference does not mean exclusivity or limitation to a single class.

In addition, the Brazilian statements show some questionable tendencies — more, perhaps, on the part of the experts than of the ecclesial base communities. Here are some of these tendencies.

1. The description of the situation prior to the rise of the ecclesial bases communities is filled with language that implies serious accusations against the Church. That prior situation appears to have been one solely of oppression, alienation, lack of awareness, and "innocence" (*SEDOC* [Oct. 1976], p. 298).

2. Earlier, the Church belonged "to the hierarchy" and seems not to have known what to do with the people (p. 303). So say the documents. But, with all their insistence that the Church is "of the people," these documents do not seem to know what to make of the hierarchy, and especially of the priests (p. 290). Two tendencies are at work with regard to the priest. One is to see no essential distinction between the ordained minister and the non-ordained, who is also described as an "extraordinary" minister (p. 278). The other tendency is to reinterpret the priesthood: the priest ceases to be the sole repository of religious power to conduct celebrations and speak in the name of God; he becomes, instead, the leader of the ecclesial community, that is, not a minister of the

sacraments but one who articulates relationships within the community (p. 290).

3. There is a tendency to eliminate the catechetical relationship between teacher and learner and to accept everyone as equally capable of interpreting the word of God in the concrete conditions of life (p. 287). This tendency is closely linked to the idea that the poor man is the true teacher and that courses in theology and centers of formation only do harm. Everything must arise from the people, and "people" means the "poor," especially Indians and blacks.

Also, one must be on guard not to form lay people who end up as a kind of mini-priest. This is the view of an expert (pp. 279–81), who seems to make his own, with little reservation, the postulates of the "Church of the People" as represented by the Christians of the left.

4. There is also a tendency to conduct religious sacramental celebrations without a priest and without reference to the possession of ecclesiastical office (p. 289). These celebrations include the Eucharist, in which the material for the eucharistic sacrifice is cocoa (at Linhares), fish (Regencia and Lagoa), coffee, etc. (cf. *SEDOC* [May 1975], pp. 1088–89). One expert goes so far as to grant lay people the power, in theory, to celebrate a "true, real, sacramental" Eucharist without an ordained minister (*SEDOC* [Oct. 1976], pp. 432–38), provided these lay people are presiding over a community that is suffering from being deprived of the Eucharist, that desires it in communion with the entire Church, "and feels moved by the Spirit to celebrate the Lord's Supper" (p. 434). But "feeling moved by the Spirit" is evidently so subjective a criterion that it is difficult to determine how it can be applied in practice. Who would be the judge, to decide whether the Holy Spirit is really moving men and authorizing a liturgical act that has been so constantly and unhesitatingly assigned to the ordained minister by the Church of which that same Holy Spirit is the soul?

II. Specifics

We now turn to a more careful and thorough examination of certain concepts, requirements, attitudes, and choices related to creation of a "Church of the People."

1. The Concept "People" and Its Attributes

The notion of "people" is obviously basic for a new church that defines itself as "popular" or "born of the people" and that wishes to be "of and for the people."

In the various statements and articles we have been citing the term "people" frequently occurs as a synonym for "the poor"; "the poor," in turn means "the oppressed," and the "oppressed" are a "class" in the Marxist sense of the word. "An option in behalf of the poor" is, in this view, "a class option.' "To choose the side of the poor is to choose for one social class and against another," said Gustavo Gutiérrez at the Escorial convention of 1972.[14]

Pablo Richard tells us that gradually "the somewhat romantic word 'poor' has been replaced by 'exploited.' The new term makes it clear that poverty results from exploitation."[15] This facile and uncritical identification of the romantic "poor" with the harsher words "exploited" and "oppressed" is based on emotion and tactical convenience rather than on scientific analysis. Its advantage is that it opens the door for the Marxist idea of "class." The same can be said of using the word "people" as though it were synonymous with "poor" and "oppressed." All who are not oppressed and therefore are not of the people automatically become oppressors and non-people.

The statement by the *Iglesia Joven* movement in 1968 (cf. no. 1 in the list of documents, above) already showed signs of this movement toward the Marxist reinterpretation of ecclesiology when it said that "people" would embrace all of mankind "if mankind were not divided into exploiters and exploited." But because mankind is so divided, "people" means "the majority of human beings, which is dominated by a minority that has usurped power." Those in power are non-people.

Commission VII of the First Latin American Convention of Christians for Socialism (held at Santiago, Chile, in April 1972) took the term "people" to include "not only those who have direct and painful experience of exploitation, but everyone who puts himself at the service of the people in their struggle" (5/p. 237). In other words, Christians for Socialism (CfS) are also "people"! Ever since then, all the Christians for Socialism make this claim, even if they are not themselves poor and oppressed.

Generally speaking, however, the documents that speak of "the people" feel no need of defining the term. Raúl Vidales is one writer who pays some attention to this point, and it will be worth our while to see how he handles it.

> When we speak of a "Church of the People" we must be careful to make it clear that we are not giving the phrase the universalist meaning it has for various populist movements (in that sense, we could speak of "the people" of Peru or Mexico or Ireland). For us, the term "people" is historically connected with the exploited sectors within a dependent capitalist system such as the one of which we are now the victims in Latin America.
>
> "The people," then, consists of those groups whose common interests are opposed to the interests of the dominant class at a

given point in the history of a country and its political conjuncture. The term thus presupposes a knowledge of who in each country are the exploiters and who the exploited; in other words, we must know who are the people and who their enemies. Given that kind of precise knowledge, we will be in a position to know how Christian love is to be manifested, since the specific characteristic of that love is that we "love our enemies" (Mt 5:43–48; Lk 6:27–28, 32–36).

Once the term "the people" is thus understood, we can go on to speak of the "popular masses" in the revolutionary sense of the words. We can also be aware of the full extent of these "masses," since the masses comprise not only "social classes" properly so called (groups which share a certain place within the system of social production; the workers, for example, and the farmers), but also all those sectors of the population that have been relegated to a socio-economic, political, and cultural position that is marginal. To believe in God is to believe in the people and to maintain that the masses have unlimited power for transforming history, in the measure that they enter upon the way of self-consciousness, organization, mobilization, and political activity in pursuit of a clearly grasped and accepted revolutionary plan.[16]

There is, however, an important nuance in this concept of the people as the oppressed (Marx's "proletariat"). When Hugo Assmann speaks of the "epistemological privilege" of the poor-as-oppressed,[17] he calls attention to the fact that it is not the oppressed person as such who is best qualified to understand and bear witness to the Gospel. In other words, the objective condition of being oppressed is not enough to make a person capable of evangelizing or of understanding God's word. The privileged position of the oppressed person, in regard both to understanding and to preaching the word, "depends upon his 'fidelity,' not in the doctrinalist sense of the word, but in its biblical sense." By this is meant that "they alone are privileged witnesses to the Gospel which they have understood and made their own, who struggle for their own liberation and who endeavor to break their own chains." If the poor man does not verify this condition of fidelity, "he does not represent the word of God that is active in history."

Francisco Vanderhoff and Miguel Angel Campos emphasize this same point and likewise regard it as extremely important:

> The sole source and only adequate environment for this liberating and transforming praxis is the people in their situation of oppression, repression, and deprivation of human rights. The people, in the sense of the proletariat, along with the groups and individuals who take seriously the cause of the people, verify the objective conditions required for thinking and acting so as to produce radical historical change.[18]

It is perhaps also to be kept in mind that the oppressed people in question are only those who are oppressed by "the bourgeoisie" or the capitalist system. The oppression caused by socialist, Communist, or Marxist systems is ignored in principle, or at least causes not the slightest concern — that those who are doing the oppressing are "the people."

We seem now to have all the elements required for the concept "people" as understood and employed by Christians for Socialism and related movements. Five conditions must be verified if there is to be a "people":

1. The persons and groups must be materially poor;
2. They must be objectively oppressed (by capitalists);
3. They must be conscious that they are being exploited;
4. They must struggle against the (capitalist) oppressors for their own liberation;
5. They must carry on this struggle in the radical form of a class struggle, as taught by the Marxists (and not in the "reformist" manner indicated in the social teaching of the Church).

"People" also includes, however, all those who, while not themselves poor or oppressed (Christians for Socialism, e.g.), "choose the side of the poor." That is, they take the side of the oppressed whose consciousness has been raised, and they share their struggle for liberation and for the establishment of a new society in which there will be neither class nor privilege nor exploitation. Only this "people" is capable of building and constituting the "Church of the People." Others — the great majority of mankind, in fact — are not the "people" and do not qualify as members of the new "Church of the People."

Quite extraordinary attributes are assigned to this "people" (which is poor and oppressed, has its consciousness raised, struggles, and liberates):

1. *Sole locus of the encounter with God.* "We meet God in the work of liberation and nowhere else. This is an undeniable datum of our experience, but I think it is not very clear in our minds. The reason for this lack of clarity is that we have become accustomed to thinking of God as present in the mind of man or in the community made up solely of believers" (7/p. 422).

2. *Sole messengers of the Gospel.* "The kingdom becomes present when the Gospel is preached to the poor, but we are convinced that this presence of the kingdom occurs in fact only when the poor themselves bring the good news of liberation to all mankind; that is, when the poor themselves make the Gospel their own and proclaim it in word and action by rejecting the society that exploits them and marginalizes them" (24/no. 16).

3. *True subject of the Church.* "To the extent that the people become the subject of history, the people of God will be the true subject of the Church" (24/no. 26). It is to be noted that this text, when taken in context, clearly means that only the poor and oppressed are the real "people of God."

4. *Prophetic privilege of the people.* If we maintain that the Church possesses authorities and individuals who are experts in theology and evangelization, we are "ideologizing" the faith. Against this kind of ideologization, "we assert the right and power of the poor to interpret and put into practice the liberating word" (25/4.2). The same document speaks of the necessity of a "social

appropriation of the Gospel": "In the base communities [the "poor," the "people"] a militant reading of the word is being effected. The poor have the sensibility and receptivity required for accepting the word of the Lord and putting it into practice as a people." Others (the "non-people") read the Bible in an "individualistic" way, whereas the poor effect a "social appropriation of the word."

Another commission at the Quebec convention speaks of "the prophetic and charismatic power of the people." It claims that the people are the "critics" of the ecclesial institution, and it rejects any leadership that would regard itself as "depository of the truth." It states, finally, that the prophetic ministry must be subject to the control of the community and must be grounded in the community (26/2.6).

Referring to the need of a "new formulation of Christianity," another document published by Christians for Socialism declares: "This [formulation] cannot be the work of a few specialists [theologians], but only of the believing community as it carries on its struggles. The community must take seriously its prophetic mission (which in the past was suppressed by the 'overseers' of the community) and understand that the charism exists despite the institution" (17/D.1.2).

According to these various statements and claims, an indispensable condition for hearing and understanding the word of God is to belong to those who are poor and oppressed and have had their consciousness raised.[19] "If the rich want to be saved, their task is not to become rich people who are good, but to cease to be rich" (13/p. 266). There seems to be no possibility of living a Christian life in a situation in which there is no poverty, oppression, and consciousness raising. When the class struggle has ceased (in a socialist society), there will be no need of Christ's Gospel, nor will any of the conditions be verified that are required for hearing it. All will be happy "new men" from the very moment of their conception in the "new society." All will be conceived without original sin. Even the "theology of liberation" will be impossible, for such a theology presupposes the existence of oppression, dependence, and captivity. But a theology that is not a "theology of liberation" is no theology at all, according to the repeated assertions of the theologians of liberation. In the new society, then, there will be no theology.[20]

5. *Missionary privilege of the people.* "We reject the manipulative practice of going out and evangelizing the people as though we were the proprietors of the truth. The people are evangelized when they begin to evangelize themselves and we share the task with them. The poor are the creators both of history and of the Church" (25/2.7).

6. *Epistemological privilege of the people.* We have already seen Hugo Assmann's statement of the great privilege the people have when it comes to understanding the word of God properly. Other texts which we have cited say pretty much the same thing. "The people as they struggle for their historical liberation are the only source to which we can look for a reasoned theological renewal of the liberating function of the symbolic system."[21] The poor are the most important theological source.[22] There is no valid theological source apart from poverty, oppression, and dependence.

7. *Sole subject of theology.* The subject that produces theological thinking can only be the same as the subject that engages in liberating praxis. This is because — according to Christians for Socialism — liberating praxis is the source, norm, and judge of truth and faith; it is the supreme theological source, and provides the horizon within which all theological thinking must be done. The primordial act out of which a theology of liberation arises is real, effective participation in the struggle for liberation of the Latin American continent.[23] "Historical praxis is the Christian tribunal; it passes judgment on the truth or falsity of faith, and from that judgment there can be no appeal" (18/1.4.2).

For this reason, says the document just quoted, the work of reformulating the Christian faith "is not something to be accomplished in a laboratory, that is, by a group of 'theologians'; the daily activity of committed Chrstians is the real school of theology"

(18/B.3). A basic element in a theological methodology proper to Latin America is a "redefinition of the agent of theology: no longer the professional theologian, but the "Christian group" or "community." This means that the subject who theologizes is a collective subject. This in turn means that the people appropriate in a new way the means of semantic production so that they may create a political theology."[24] In other words, socialized theology! "Only the proletariat can translate the struggle for liberation into credible theological terms, in a rational way that is more scientific and constructive."[25]

Raúl Vidales draws the pious conclusion that "there is only one basic stance possible for the theologian: his work must be based on, and be in the service of, the poor."[26] In a series of conferences on faith and politics in Bogota in April 1976, Mario Peresson S.D.B. gave a talk that was titled "The Community of Christians Committed to the Struggle for the Liberation of the Oppressed: Sole Agent of the Theology of Liberation."

Anything else must necessarily be a "theology of domination."

2. Serious Accusations against the Church

All the zeal and energy expended in behalf of a "new Church" is accompanied by a deep discontent with the one, holy, catholic Church as it now exists. The discontent finds expression throughout the documents we have been studying. These theologians are not satisfied to say, with the Second Vatican Council, that the Church reveals the mystery of the Lord in only a "shadowed" way (*LG,* 8e/24), or that she "is at the same time holy and always in need of being purified" (*LG,* 8d/24), or that her sons must "purify and renew themselves" (*LG*, 15b/34), or even that in her present state "the Holy Spirit . . . renews and purifies her ceaselessly" (*GS* 21e/219), although, at the same time, "by the power of the Holy Spirit the Church has remained the faithful spouse of the Lord" (*GS*, 43j/245) and "is faithful to the truth of the Gospel" (*DH*, 12a/692).

This doctrine of the Church's substantial fidelity to the will, intentions, and teaching of her Spouse, Lord, and Master is denied by those who want a "new Church of the People." They claim, over and over again, that the Church is at the service of the bourgeoisie, that it is allied with the bourgeoisie, that it is subject to manipulation by the bourgeoisie; that it is an instrument for controlling the people — that is, it is in the hands of individuals who are allied with the national and international bourgeoisie; that the Christianity it preaches is linked, ideologically and structurally, with the ruling system; that it adopts the interests of the ruling classes; that it has been taken over by the ruling powers and used as an ideological instrument for perpetuating the status quo; that it is the ideological division of the state; and so on and so on.

It is not worth citing the texts and their sources beyond one example: "Christianity is an organism that serves the capitalist system. Not only has the Church entered into a covenant with the ruling system; it also serves as a laboratory for working out moral concepts that will determine and breed behavior which serves the interests of the capitalist system" (18/2.2.2).

It must be noted that in this and similar texts the accusation is couched in very general terms. It is not simply certain individuals in the Church, or some category of Church members, but the Church as such, without qualification, that stands in the dock.

Much more serious, however, are the charges that the Church has been unfaithful to the Gospel (19/132); that from the viewpoint of the Gospel it is illegitimate (18/1.43); that it possesses no Christian legitimacy (18/13.3); that its tradition has been "unclear, erroneous, or off the track" (18/2.2.3); that its Christianity is a deformation (16/no. 42); that it has stripped the Gospel of its power (15/p. 22); that it has perverted the Gospel (20/introd.); that it has perverted its own mission (20/46); that it has betrayed both the people and the Gospel (21/2.3.3). "The

Church has lost its grip on the Gospel message; it has become so institutionalized that its message has lost its legitimacy and global verification, even though the Church continues its claim of universality."[27]

In the language of the documents we are studying, the Gospel, the Christian faith, and Christianity have been ideologized, sequestered, domesticated, deformed, stripped of power, degraded, led astray, manipulated, depoliticized, privatized, and monopolized.

The key word, however, and the one that says it all for these people is "ideologized." The most frequently heard accusation is that the faith has been "ideologized." Consequently, the chief task is to *de*ideologize the faith, and the most important undertaking — one that is proclaimed over and over — is the "ideological struggle" within the Church itself.

The word "ideology," though used so frequently, is nonetheless never defined.[28] Only Gonzalo Arroyo comes out and says that "it is a rather ambiguous and difficult word" (8/pp. 376–77). It can be said, however, that throughout these documents the word always has a pejorative meaning, which can be summed up thus: "ideology" is everything that conceals and distorts reality and protects the interests of the privileged. Its function is to justify power and privilege, and to conceal the conflict that is being waged in history. More simply, its function is to rationalize and justify a given system. Gustavo Gutiérrez explains: "At bottom, ideology camouflages reality and creates an illusion; it yields knowledge that is unauthentic."[29]

"Ideology," with this pejorative meaning, is applied to the faith. An "ideologized faith" is a faith that is unauthentic and illusory, that hides reality, that justifies the interests of the privileged that conceals the reality of the class struggle. To assert that the Church has "ideologized the faith" evidently implies a serious accusation of perversity and wickedness on the part of the Church.

By way of summing everything up, Christians who use Marxist tools of analysis can make no statement more wounding than "the Church is a superstructure" (5/p. 208). In the Marxist view, a "superstructure" is a set of alienating factors, with the help of which capitalism seeks to make men, and especially the proletariat, prisoners, so that it may more easily rule and exploit them.

In consequence, "this process is closely connected with an alienation of the Church. We are not rejecting the Church as such, but the historical causes and conditions of the Church, as expressed in its declarations, teachings, activities, etc."[30]

But if one rejects all that, what is left of the Church?

Despite this attitude to the Church, these people solemnly assert:

> As Christians committed to a Marxist-revolutionary struggle, we proclaim our membership in the Church, and we are unwilling to be marginalized and forced to act clandestinely within the Church [16/no. 54]. Proceeding by action and analysis, we will also solve all the problems raised by our intention of being daily both more Christian and more Marxist, and of having an ever greater right to a place in the Church while also manning with increasing effectiveness our post on the socialist front [21/43].

3. Liberation of Consciences

One of the most urgent tasks in the creation of a "Church of the People" is "the liberation of the Christian masses from ideology." According to Christians for Socialism, the conscience of the Christian people is hindered by an ideologized faith and morality from liberating the energies needed for exerting revolutionary means: kidnaping, guerrilla warfare, etc. Almost all the documents emphasize the need of "liberating consciences." The Cuban report at the First Latin American Convention of Christians for Socialism emphasizes this point:

> It is necessary to eradicate the moral and dogmatic setting of

> norms which deadens political, social, and economic activity of a satisfactory sort. Utilizing the inner springs of our spirituality, which were dried up but have begun to well up in our contact with the revolutionary process, we seek to replace outmoded normative elements of a dogmatic sort with normative elements deriving from the real-life context. The Incarnation points us in that direction, a direction that accords with the historical moment in which we are living.[31]

At the same convention, the Third Commission (5/no. 1.2) polemicizes against "the puritanical moralism that is the fruit of a bourgeois morality" and that makes it difficult for people to engage in political work with its requirements and strategies. "Participation in the struggle of the people enables men to overcome bourgeois moralism and to make use of revolutionary means which those outside the movement cannot understand." The Seventh Commission, at the same convention, asserted that the Christian must continue "to be marked by a freedom that is conditioned solely by the law of love for the neighbor, and by an unremitting rejection of every other concept of legality. All these other concepts, as conveyed through teachings, norms, doctrines, etc., only hide the Christian's calling to faith and a love characterized by freedom" (5/6.1.3).

Another document explains the liberation as follows:

> At the level of the masses, and on every platform available to us, we must make our experience and method known, and thus directly combat the bourgeois ideology that has saturated the faith of a somnolent people and has paralyzed it when revolutionary choices are to be made. At the same time, we must stir up those possessing charisms and lead them to commitment and practice in the service of the socialist front, convincing them that only by "doing" will they reach full "understanding" [21/no. 23.2].

Our faith, says another document, "is not exhausted by making a political choice, but acquires its real, concrete expression only in the revolutionary struggle. This conviction must supply the impulse for taking up a very important task: that of blocking the influence of the official religious ideology which denies believers the possibility of a radical commitment to the people. In every place, therefore, where Christians share their faith, we must see to it that our experience and method guide the attainment of awareness and the class choice made by many Christians now committed to the bourgeoisie" (19/19.2). This method of liberating consciences "is the starting point for a reformulation of Christianity," according to another document (18/2.2.3).

The end result of this violent manner of "liberating consciences" will evidently be a new morality and, especially, a new concept of sin. The report of a "Reinterpretation of the Faith" workshop (Spain, 1976) tells us: "A majority of the group asserted that they had overcome a sense of sin that was based on the failure to live by determined norms" (34/p. 26).

Undoubtedly, a remarkable "liberation" has already occurred.

4. Reinterpretation of the Faith

Reinterpretation of the faith is another step that is regarded as indispensable and as a pressing need in the establishment of the new "Church of the People." According to a conviction shared by all who are working for this "new Church," the faith we have inherited is a faith that has been ideologized, domesticated, deformed, etc., etc. Therefore they urge, in their words, a "deideologization of the faith," a "reinterpretation of the faith," a "transformation of the faith," a "reformulation of the faith," a "purification of the faith," a "rereading of the faith," a "restatement of the faith," a "new expression of the faith." "The Christian conscience of the Christians for Socialism regards political emancipation as a challenge that casts suspicion on the entire dogmatic teaching of the institutional Church" (18/1.4).

A "scientific analysis of reality," according to the Marxist method, is an absolutely necessary condition for a correct understanding of what Christians for Socialsm calls "faith." Such an approach leads its members to suspect that almost all the content of the faith, and its formulations, have been "ideologized" and to "regard the ideological struggle as essential." This was asserted at the First Convention in Santiago, Chile (4/II.2). According to the final document issued at this convention (chap. 2, sec. 2 of "Christianity and the Ideological Struggle"), to propose a Christian social doctrine is to ideologize; to insist that there are natural laws or to speak of human nature or the natural needs of human society is to ideologize; to speak of man as an individual or person with individual capacities, tasks, and destinies is to ideologize; to emphasize the spiritual side of man or moral ideas and attitudes is to ideologize; to describe diversities, dependences, the division of labor, and privileges as forms of pluralism and complementarity that are required by order and the common good is to ideologize; to advocate collaboration and dialogue between classes and peoples is to ideologize.

The final statement of the Second International Convention of Christians for Socialism, at Quebec (24/nos. 21–23), pursues the same line: to promote the spiritual and to assert the transcendence of the spiritual is to ideologize. We find similar statements in the other documents: to speak of unity, peace, reconciliation, nonviolence, love of enemies, Christian resignation, authority from God, is to ideologize (5/p. 230). Everything must be deideologized — which comes down to saying that everything must simply be rejected.

If we were to adopt the mentality and logic of these deideologizers of the faith, we would have to say that when Jesus Christ recommended humility, reconciliation, forgiveness, and love of enemies, he was ideologizing; when he spoke of the Father and his divine providence, he was ideologizing; when he promised recompense after death, he was ideologizing; when St. Matthew interpreted the poor of Luke 6:20 as the "poor in spirit" (Mt

5:3), he was ideologizing; when the same evangelist explained that the hungry (Lk 6:21) are those who "hunger and thirst for justice" (Mt 5:6), he was ideologizing; when St. Paul urged the Romans to submit to established authority (Rom 13:1), he was ideologizing; when he bade the slaves of Ephesus or Colossae to obey their masters with reverence, awe, and sincerity (Eph 6:5–9, Col 3:22–25), he was ideologizing; when he told the Philippians, with tears, that unlike those who think only of earthly things, "we have our citizenship in heaven" (Phil 3:17–21), he was ideologizing. All these people were "bourgeois."

It is simply not in accord with historical fact to claim that "ideologically the Christian faith, via the structure of the Church, is part of bourgeois society" (5/p. 229). Such, nonetheless, is the starting point of those who claim the power or competence to "reformulate the faith in behalf of the Church of the People."

The final statement of the Quebec meeting is the most authoritative expression thus far of this group. The whole of the chapter "The New Practice of the Faith" (24/nn. 15–19) should be analyzed, but no. 18 contains statements so inordinate "that one asks by what gradual stages any Christian could have come to them without being aware of the radical metamorphosis of the Christian faith that they imply."[32] No. 18 runs as follows.

> The faith has been lived and conceived in a world that is not the world of modern revolutionary experience, a world alien to the vision of history as dialectic and involving conflict. To the extent, however, that revolutionary Christians see identification with the interests and struggles of the popular classes as being the focal point of a new way of being human and receiving the gift of the Lord's word, the awareness will come that a reflection on the faith which takes historical praxis as its starting point will be a theology which is linked to the struggle of the exploited in behalf of their freedom. It will be a militant theology based on a class option and using the same rational methods we use for analyzing and changing history. Consequently, we see the importance of Marxism in the task of reformulating and reunderstanding the

faith. In the last analysis, the truth of theology is tested by deeds, by revolutionary praxis. It is this and not mere assertions or new theoretical models that will free us from all forms of idealism.

This text is telling us that a faith lived in a nonrevolutionary world, in a world that lacks the "vision of history" as dialectical and based on conflict (in short, the Marxist vision), will inevitably be an "ideologized" faith. This means that the faith, as lived before the Marxist vision of history, was an inauthentic faith that created illusions, masked reality, justified the interests of the privileged, and concealed the class struggle. In other words, until our time there was no autheentic faith, or even the possibility of an authentic faith, because the authenticity of faith depends on knowledge of the Marxist method for analyzing and transforming history, and because the truth of the faith is created by the very actions of revolutionary praxis and is not received from outside ourselves, much less through the assertions of ecumenical councils. The key to the "new way" of receiving the gift of God's word and of doing "authentic" theology — a "militant theology" or a certain "theology of liberation" — is identification with the interests of the people and their struggle for liberation. This "historical praxis," based on a class option (for one class and against another) and on the use of the Marxist tools of analysis, is said to be the sole starting point for a true and authentic reformulation of the understanding of the faith and therefore of the faith itself.

Everything depends, evidently, on the concept of faith.

For us who belong to the ancient but ever living and dynamic Catholic Church, faith is a response of a man who surrenders himself wholly and freely to God and offers him the unrestricted homage of his mind and will by a free assent to what God reveals in "public divine revelation" as set down in sacred Scripture and sacred tradition and transmitted by the apostles and their successors. God intended, moreover, that what he revealed for the salvation of all mankind should be preserved in its fullness and passed on to all generations. In order that this divine public revelation might always be preserved living and entire in the Church, the apostles appointed successors, namely the bishops, and gave them the office of teaching. The teaching office, or magisterium, does not "stand over" the word of God but is at its service and teaches only what has been handed on. By divine mandate and with the help of the Holy Spirit, those who are empowered to teach listen devotedly to what has been handed on, guard it jealously, and explain it faithfully. Since this public revelation reached its climax in Christ and received its perfect form in him, we must not expect further public revelation until the glorious manifestation of Jesus Christ our Lord, nor can the teaching authority accept any new public revelation as belonging to the divine deposit of faith.

All this, which is nothing but a brief summary of the teaching of the most recent ecumenical council, Vatican II, is roundly denied by those who look for a new "Church of the People." In their view, the demon of ideologization led the Church of past times into infidelity and a perversion of the faith.

If we take these people seriously, everything must be begun again: reformulated, redefined, reinterpreted, restated. The Church of the past was mistaken in its very point of departure, for it started with divine public revelation. The new starting point is, and must be, solely the people of today, that is, the poor and oppressed who have had their consciousness raised — who have their liberative praxis, their concrete experience, their daily reality here and now, their revolutionary commitment, their "politics." "Politics is the basic element in faith" (18/1.4); "the evangelical message will find its fulfillment in its political expression" (18/1.4.2); "politics and the political are a basic element of being a Christian" (18/1.4.3).

"Reformulating the faith," which is the primary task of Christians for Socialism according to one document (21/23.1), is explained as follows. "It means taking the ideological struggle into ourselves. On the basis of our revolutionary experience and of the questions which Marxist science formulates for us, we must endeavor to free our faith from all bourgeois ideological influence and reformulate it in a language which must never again be abandoned: that of the oppressed and exploited, the language of liberation." The Christians for Socialism (CfS) who gathered at Bologna were well aware of this:

> Faith necessarily finds expression in relation to a project for man and society, without ever being reduced to such a project. It makes a choice between the human projects that are offered, but it never lies beyond such projects. Any attempt to locate the faith outside of human cultures and social conflicts is illusory.

In a series of conferences on faith and politics at Bogotá in April 1976, Rafael Eduardo Torrado proved himself an apt student in this new school of theology, when, in his lecture "Theology in History and in — and on the Basis of — Latin America," he said:

> Traditional theology, as cultivated in Europe, was based essentially on revealed truths which were regarded as eternal and immutable truths that came "from outside." . . . Latin American theology is being developed with historical reality as the source of God's revelation. It follows that theology is not a *logos* about God, but a *logos* on the relations between God and man. These are accessible to us, however, only in the relations between man and man. The Bible often tells us that man is the only [sic!] mediator for the encounter with God, and that the encounter with God is an encounter with man and, concretely, with the poor man. To love God and to love man are identical [*sic!*]. The man–man relationship is constitutive of history; consequently, theology is a reflection (a *logos*) on historical reality as seen in the perspective of faith.

In consequence, this faith is identified with liberative political praxis.

Torrado gives a further explanation of the thinking of the theological school to which he belongs: "Faith is not an intellectual adhesion to certain truths, but the response of commitment to a truth that is taking shape (praxis) in history. . . . The specific contribution of a Latin American theology is to have shown, in and on the basis of praxis, that faith is a praxis of liberation." "Faith is the starting point inasmuch as it supplies motivation and is a critical reflection on human praxis, a reflection that becomes ever more concrete through a continual search and through praxis itself. Consequently, 'the perspective of faith' means an option concerning praxis, but an option that can be made only on the basis of praxis itself."

Praxis! Praxis is *the new theological source.* This is implicit in all that we have seen, and the final statement of the Quebec convention says it in so many words: "Many of us Christians have discovered that commitment to historical, liberating, revolutionary praxis is the source of experience, reflection, communication, and celebration of our faith in Christ. Christ has enabled us to see ever more clearly that the revolutionary task is the place where faith attains its true dimensions and its radically subversive power" (24/no. 15). This is the teaching of Gustavo Gutiérrez: "It is within the class struggle to which a Christian must necessarily be committed, and within the historical praxis of subversive liberation that a place is to be found for encountering the Lord, and this locus is theological."[33]

It is perfectly acceptable, of course, to say that liberating or revolutionary historical praxis may be a means of discovering new demands or dimensions of faith, just as other human situations (suffering joy, etc.) may be. In any event, this does not turn praxis (or any other situation) into a theological source in the proper sense, but into a hermeneutical source or locus. Some go so far as to claim that praxis is not only the theological source par excellence but even the *only* theological source.

"Praxis" is a word in constant use. As can be seen from the numerous texts we have quoted, the word has a rather reductionist meaning: it refers solely to *liberating revolutionary action that transforms reality.* In general, however, we do not find any great desire to provide definitions or to explain notions and concepts.

For these heirs of existentialism, knowledge of the essence of things holds no great interest.

For example, let us take Gustavo Gutiérrez' *Theology of Liberation,*[34] which, at the beginning, presents theology as "critical reflection on praxis" (p. 6). Despite the evident importance of the word "praxis" for this "new way of theologizing," it is used without any effort to define its meaning. On pages 6–7 we get the impression that what is meant is simply "Christian praxis," that is, the faith that finds expression in loving dedication to God and neighbor. Suddenly, however, a few pages later, the word reappears, but it now has the Marxist meaning: transformation of the world, and man's action in history (p. 27). "Historical practice" (p. 6 and, title of a subsection) is now political work. However, the language continues to be quite vague. On page 10, praxis, in the sense of "the transformation of the world," is presented, without further ado, as the criterion for "veri-fying" our faith, that is, for "doing the truth." Then, unexpectedly, the expression "praxis of liberation" appears (p. 14), with the assertion that we need a theology based on liberating praxis, that is, a "theology of liberation." This praxis of liberation on which theology must critically reflect now has the Marxist meaning of "transforming praxis" (cf. p. 15). Later, Gutiérrez speaks of "social praxis" (p. 46) and asserts that it is "the arena in which the Christian works out — along with others — both his destiny as man and his life of faith in the Lord of history" (p. 49). This leads to the affirmation of the primacy of the political.

Pablo Richard explains to European theologians that the Latin American theology of liberation takes as the starting point for theological work not an analysis or interpretation of reality but the transformation of reality, that is, praxis.[35] Reality can be analyzed and interpreted only to the extent that we transform it. If theology wants knowledge of reality for its starting point, it must share in the process of transforming this reality. Theological work must even become a praxis of liberation, a specifically liberating moment in a comprehensive praxis of liberation that is economic, political, cultural, and religious. Consequently, the primordial and originating act of the theology of liberation is to participate in a real and effective way in the struggle for liberation on the Latin American continent.

Praxis is the *new starting point* — so say the leaders of the Federation of Latin American Priests' Movements:

> Political praxis enables us to share the transforming power of history, and bids us make our own the project of liberating the Latin American proletariat. This praxis enables us to discover anew God present and acting in history; we reexperience the great evangelical values of love, justice, and action on behalf of the most underprivileged members of society; there takes place a deideologization of the Gospel message, which a culture bent on oppression has used and deformed [14/II.B.2].

Praxis is the *new criterion of truth.* "The theology of liberation cannot but assign a privileged place to praxis as the criterion of historical and evangelical truth." "Given the perspective of liberation, theological discourse allots the Christian praxis of liberation a privileged place as interpretative matrix, first word in theology, and first moment in the interpretation and rereading of the Lord's word."[36]

Speaking of the theologian of liberation, Mario Peresson tells us: "His criterion of ultimate truth will not be agreement or disagreement with pregiven doctrines, but effectiveness in transforming history and liberating the oppressed; that is, orthopraxis."[37] It is evident that "agreement with pregiven doctrines" is unimportant; such a criterion is characteristic of "European theology." Latin-americanized theology[38] is different and has adopted a different criterion. As Jon Sobrino told the Latin American theologians in Mexico City, "European theology started with the presupposition that there is a deposit of truth or at least of meanings that must be passed on, interpreted, and made meaningful." "Latin American theology, insofar as it is a theological knowledge, starts with different presuppositions. . . . It arose out of an experienced praxis of liberation."[39]

Praxis is the *new infallible magisterium.* "If this political praxis is the essence of Christianity, then it is also the tribunal at which judgment is passed on the truth or falsity of the dogmas which have left their mark on the history of the Church. When we say that politics is the basic constituent of faith, we are saying, above all, that *historical praxis is the Christian tribunal of final instance for judging the truth or falsity of the faith.* Faith in its different forms ceases to be an inviolable area and becomes subject to the inclemencies of time. Its legitimacy depends on its political influence as measured in the perspective of the interests of the poor" (18/1.4.2; italics in the original).

Praxis is the *new evangelization.* Accept revolutionary practice and you are a Christian. In July 1973, at a National Chilean Workshop, Christians for Socialism passed a resolution: "In contrast with a Christianity bent on domination, we assert a Christ who liberates, and we link Christianity with the revolution, so that the people are automatically Christians when they are engaged in the struggle."[40] At Quebec in 1975, this declaration was made: "We now understand better the ecclesial and evangelizing value of praxis. . . . But we are not naive: not every kind of political work is evangelizing, though it may seem effective. For example, unless the poor become the agents of historical transformation, a political praxis is not evangelizing" (25/3.5).

Because it is so important, we must dwell on this "starting point for theology" and see what the new theologians of the "Church of the People" think about it. We must be clear on this:

> The starting point for our reflections is not anything "christian." . . . The basis, rather, is revolutionary practice, the activity of the revolutionary people as they struggle to promote a socialist liberation. Consequently, we theologize without starting with "the Christian thing." Such a basis may seem alien; it may seem to be incompatible with the Gospel and the tradition of the Church. Yet,

> at bottom, it is the only procedure that is in fact faithful to the Gospel and tradition. For there can be no Christian reflection except on the struggle of the oppressed to obtain their liberation [7/p. 420].

However much these theologians may seek to get to the bottom of things, and however much they may repeat that this unrelated point of departure is not contrary to the Gospel or opposed to tradition, it is utterly opposed to everything the holy Church teaches us. This rather surprising emphasis on a non-Christian point of departure has been extensively developed by one of the first and most important ideologues of Christians for Socialism, Pablo Richard, in an essay titled "The Denial of the 'Christian Thing' as an Affirmation of Faith."[41] Here he defends the view that the starting point of theology should be nontheological. We should not start, he says, with sociological analysis that is Christian in its inspiration, nor should we follow Christian norms.

> Any attempt to preserve my Christian or theological viewpoint will prevent my adopting a point of view which enables me to become conscious of the historical mediations and conditionings of my faith. Any attempt to retain my specifically Christian identity will prevent me from seeing it through new eyes by becoming aware of all that conditions me historically. I repeat what I said earlier: you find the specifically Christian only when you cease to look for what you think of as your own specificity.

A little further on, he returns to the point: "I emphasize that the starting point is not faith or the Gospel or any other ecclesial or theological starting point. These shed no light on the constitutive elements in the political consciousness of Christians. We must start from the infrastructure, the political struggle, the class consciousness."

There is another very important element in the point of departure for the new theology, and it is worth repeating some words from a passage (earlier cited) of Rafael Eduardo Torrado, for it expresses a viewpoint commonly found in promoters of the "Church of the People," but not always so explicitly formulated. "In Latin America theology is being developed with historical reality as the source of God's revelation."[42] In other words, historical reality or the very history of our peoples is "the source of divine revelation."

In an essay, "The Catechesis of Events," written by a group of student-priests at the Latin American Pastoral Institute for Youth (IPLAJ) of Bogotá,[43] the writers insist on the principle that "history is the sole theological source of divine revelation." From this principle they immediately draw an important conclusion: "God's revelation is not a finished fact, something that ended with the glorious death of Christ." They assert that "God continues to reveal himself and to communicate with men through events." In addition, "the revelation of God is not to be found in dogmatic formulas"; consequently, "the concept of the transmission of the message, with regard to its content, disappears." They even go so far as to say: "Just as the historical events affecting the people of Israel were salvific events for them, so the historical events affecting us today have *equal value, privilege, and right* in the plan of salvation. Each people has its own saving events, its own history of salvation, and it must read and interpret this" (italics added).

Here we have in brief form a hermeneutical principle with vast theological and catechetical implications. It is presupposed, when not expressly formulated, in the entire documentation we have been studying.

Although we have not reached the point in this essay for proposing systematic, critical comments on what the new populist theologians are telling us, it is necessary to make some brief remarks that will clarify the ambiguities and dangers of this new hermeneutical principle.

When we speak of the "revelation" of God "in history," we must be clear on just what "revelation" and what "history" we are talking about. Sound Catholic theology distinguishes between "natural" revelation (the creator "reveals" himself in his creation) and "positive" revelation, which comes through "God speaking" as is found in the "word of God" in the narrower and proper sense. Within positive revelation, moreover, we usually distinguish between "public" positive revelation and "private" positive revelation. Only divine positive and public revelation (the expression "public revelation" occurs in *LG,* 25g, and *DV,* 4b) can be said to be constitutive and originative for the Christian faith and its doctrinal content. Sound Catholic theology, as commonly taught even today, also tells us that this divine positive and public revelation takes place "in history" but exclusively in "biblical" history, and reaches its culmination and conclusion in Jesus Christ, the mediator in whom the plenitude of public revelation is to be found. It is precisely this divine, positive, and public revelation that is the starting point for our faith and for our reflection on the faith (i.e., our theology), even in Latin America.

We can therefore see only folly and an utter lack of theological seriousness in the desire to make the present history of our peoples a source of true revelation that will be constitutive and originative for the Christian faith, and to claim that such a history is on a par of "value, privilege, and right" with the history of Israel. The same judgment must be passed on the vain effort to turn contemporary liberative and revolutionary praxis into a "theological source," even though we may well assign this praxis a value as a "hermeneutical source," which is something completely different.

This, however, is how the supposed reformulation of the faith is to be effected. Revelation becomes the present history of each people. The criterion by which to judge true faith becomes revolutionary, liberative praxis. The subject of faith becomes the people: poor, oppressed, and engaged in struggle after their consciousness has been raised. The method: Marxist analysis. The mediator: the social sciences. The condition for it: the class option. And its results?

The Latin American journal for pastoral matters, *Pastoral Popular*,[44] provided space for making public the results of a workshop, "Reinterpreting the Faith," which was held "in Spain, during 1976" (no further indication of place, date, or participants). As a matter of fact, the "workshop" was simply another meeting of Christians for Socialism. The "document" (that is what the periodical calls it) is a concrete example of doctrinal confusion. It gives the impression that a group of Christians met, and tried to forget everything they had learned, but were unable even to accomplish that much, at least not uniformly or equally at every point. The themes discussed were Christian hope, sin, prayer, and the Eucharist.

In speaking of *hope*, the document says that Christian hope "is not the bourgeois hope in another life that begins at death, but a hope that can be maintained only amid struggle, a hope that must take shape anew each day." For this reason, "no differences in daily practice" are to be found between a Marxist militant who is a believer and another who is not a believer. "It also became clear that for the majority of the group there is no incompatibility between faith and the carrying on of the Marxist struggle." Many "found it unnecessary to believe in a future life"; "they are not concerned about the problem of the future life."

On *sin*, the participants showed that they were very much liberated and deideologized. "A majority of the group asserted that they had overcome a sense of sin that was based on the failure to live by determined norms."

When it came to *prayer*, the group was still divided. Some felt that prayer is vitally necessary. "Others, however, felt strong resistance to prayer. In their experience, prayer has become empty of any content, while praxis and intimate communication with their fellows was filling the vacuum prayer had formerly filled." In addition, "some did not believe in the reality of a personal God."

As for the *Eucharist*, "almost all rejected the traditional parish and the Eucharist as celebrated in that framework." Is a priest needed for the Eucharist? "One group said they celebrated the

Eucharist without a priest and had been doing so for some time, since we are all priests."

From these examples it is clear that the "reinterpretation" of the faith, as here proposed, is not and does not seek to be a simple "reformulation" of the perennial content of the faith so as to make it better adapted to the condition and capacity for understanding poor and oppressed people. Such a reformulation, of course, is something we all regard as necessary, which the Second Vatican Council says is "the law of all evangelization" (*GS,* 44c/246).

Evidently, the concern in such a "reinterpretation" is not simply to give the participants the opportunity to express themselves freely, as every Catholic has the right to do, in what are called "disputed questions." Whether there is a future life, whether we are obliged to obey the commandments of God, and whether we can celebrate the Eucharist without an ordained minister are not something the members of the Catholic Church find open to discussion. There is only one answer to each of these questions, and that answer is a dogma or article of faith. Denial is heresy, even if one prefers to call the denial a "reformulation."

Further examples of this type could easily be supplied, such as the statements of this group on ecclesiology (the subject we have chiefly been concentrating on). The document makes it evident that "reinterpretation" almost always means denial or qualitative change (the "qualitative leap" they boast of).

They deny the substantial fidelity of Christ's Spouse to the Gospel, as well as her integral and incorrupt transmission of the Gospel through the ages, since they accuse her of having "ideologized" the faith. They introduce a "qualitative change" into the mission of the Church when they bid her mobilize the masses in favor of a specific kind of revolution and when they identify evangelization with the praxis of liberation and revolution. They change the concept of "people of God" when they identify it exclusively with the poor and exploited who have had their consciousness raised. They introduce a new concept of the ecclesiastical magisterium, and assign the teaching office to a new agent, when they attribute to the poor and oppressed all prophetic and missionary privileges, and all privileged knowledge, in relation to the proclamation and understanding of the word of God, and when they assert that the poor and oppressed are the sole evangelizers and the sole subject of theology. They change the conditions for belonging to the Church when they set down, as an indispensable condition, the commitment to one class and to the struggle of this one class against the other. They transform the very concept of the unity of the Church when they teach that this unity must take second place to the socialist unity of mankind.

Such denials, changes, and qualitative leaps also occur in the concept of faith (we have seen in the texts), for faith is identified with a political commitment to liberation, so that an individual has the Christian faith by the very fact that he commits himself, within ongoing history, to the liberation of the oppressed. He is a "Christian believer," even though he rejects the qualitatively new and transcendent content of divine public revelation. An important "qualitative" leap is also made in the concept of revelation, since the historical source of the Latin American peoples is *the* theological source, that is, the source of God's constitutive revelation to us.

In this fashion the Christians for Socialism go about changing or denying the whole traditional content of our holy faith. They use the language of classical theology but fill it with a different meaning, which confuses and perplexes the uninitiated. Charity, conversion, salvation, liberation, grace, prophecy, new man, word of God, sin, solidarity, brotherhood, dignity, dualism, the unity of history: all these words and phrases receive a qualitatively new meaning in this "reformulation" of the faith. Insofar as these people are still correct, they are unoriginal; where they are original, they are wrong.

Properly understood, this complex "restatement" of the faith raises a problem of theological epistemology and pertains to Fundamental Theology. As a matter of fact, all the innovative positions and demands for a "reformulation" of the faith are based on five epistemological presuppositions that deserve critical study:

1. Praxis is a source or (theological) locus of truth or of "doing" the truth; it is also a criterion for and judge of truth.
2. History (present history and the history of each people) is a source of (constitutive) divine revelation.
3. The class option is an indispensable condition for reaching the truth.
4. The people (i.e., the oppressed who have had their consciousness raised) are the bearers of the Gospel, the subject of all theologizing, and sole locus for the encounter with God.
5. The social sciences (and especially Marxist analysis) mediate the truth.

5. Rereading the Bible

According to Christians for Socialism at the First Latin American Convention, this new kind of theological reflection, which is based on revolutionary praxis (understood as "the matrix that will generate a new theological creativity"),

> leads the Christian, in a spirit of authentic [i.e., not "ideologized"] faith, to a new reading of the Bible and Christian tradition. It poses the basic concepts and symbols of Christianity anew, in such a way that they do not hamper Christians in their commitment to the revolutionary process but rather help them to shoulder these commitments in a creative way [4/II.3.7–8].[45]

At the Second International Convention in Quebec, the Second Commission stated that unless we are engaged in the class struggle there is no way for the word of God to put its questions to us: "A re-reading of the Bible also takes place in the light of this classist praxis. By thus locating the re-reading within the class struggle, we are not unduly instrumentalizing the word of God but simply creating the condition required if the word of God is to dispute the truth with us" (26/2.5).

The 3,000 Christians for Socialism who gathered at Bologna felt the same way:

> We can live in fidelity to both Christ and the poor only through a vital revolutionary commitment. When we make that commitment, we discover an entirely new way of reading the Bible. . . . This is an immense task, to rediscover the original meaning of the Gospel and its suppressed virtualities; it is a task to which we feel ourselves collectively obliged. We look on it as a reappropriation of the Gospel by the poor to whom it belongs and from whom it has been taken by force [22/p. 337].

One of the most persistent propagandists of Christians for Socialism, the Chilean priest Esteban Torres, asserts pontifically that a "bourgeois" reading of the Bible is not only ideological and false but "is an idolatrous reading, an atheistic reading, a false search for God." In his view, the only correct reading must be based on a class option in behalf of the oppressed. In this area, there can be no pluralism; to admit a pluralism here is a "deviation."[46]

We have already cited "routine" examples of the kind of rereading of the Bible that the founders of the new "Church of the People" are looking for or postulating; but in 1973 Fernando Belo, a Portuguese, published *A Materialist Reading of the Gospel of Mark in French.* The Catholic publisher who published it in Spanish[47] recommended it with these words: "The Gospel of Mark is an account of a practice that is radically subversive. The subversive aspect of the account has been obscured for centuries by an idealist and bourgeois exegesis. This must now be counteracted by a materialist reading."

Here again we have the same vigorous zeal to debourgeoisify

and deideologize, but now the Bible itself is submitted to the process. The criterion is always the same: Be subversive, and start with a revolutionary praxis based on Marxist methods, and you will achieve authenticity.

In its August–September (no. 10) 1976 issue, *Liaisons Internationales,* the international organ of Christians for Socialism, published an essay titled "A Materialist Interpretation of Luke 6:20, 24, and Matthew 5:3." The introduction tells us: "The materialist interpretation of biblical texts is becoming increasingly important for the theoretical work of Christians for Socialism. This kind of interpretation does not start from the texts and draw arguments from them that will be the basis for a political praxis; the starting point is rather concrete action in historical situations of class struggle. The texts are the *expression* of these situations."

Now we hear of a "Latin American reading of the Bible."[48] In 1976, Everardo Ramírez Toro published his *Evangelio Latinoamericano de la Liberación* and described it as a "new translation of the Gospel of Jesus."[49] The author is persuaded that his version has restored the original meaning of the Gospel and has rescued the person and message of Jesus from all the mystifications of the centuries. "Now, for the first time, men will read the Gospel in its original meaning, without the confusions and deviations produced by vested interests" (p. 10).

Here, for example, is how this "translation" handles the birth of Jesus:

> Before Joseph began to live with Mary, the mother of Jesus, whom he had taken as his wife, he became aware that she was pregnant. Being a just man of the people, and one who loved Mary and did not want to destroy her reputation, Joseph decided to give her up without saying anything to anyone. But during the night he had a dream, and he heard a voice saying to him: "Joseph, son of the people, do not hesitate to take Mary as your wife, for she is innocent and has not been violated" [p. 13].

The enemies of Jesus refer to his obscure origins: "Our origins are pure, unlike yours, for you are a natural child, and no one knows who your real Father was." To which Jesus replies: "Who of you can accuse me of anything, except for my origins, for which I was not responsible?" (p. 58). Again:

> Some reactionary and traditionalist parish priests approached Jesus to lay a trap for him; they asked him: "In the eyes of Holy Mother Church marriage is indissoluble, but many young priests, who call themselves revolutionaries, defend divorce in cases of temperamental incompatibility. What do you say to this?" Jesus answered . . . : "You hypocrites think that a religious ceremony can unite two persons for the remainder of their lives without any other factors having to be taken into account. Fools! The only thing that can inseparably unite a man and a woman is love. If two persons do not love or understand one another, why should they remain united? Let them provide for the children and separate" [p. 49].

On the same page, Jesus is asked: "What do you think of priestly celibacy?" Jesus answers: "Hypocrites! You profess chastity in public, but, within, you are full of sexual desires; you make a show of renunciation, but in secret you are worse than others. You condemn as evil what God created good, and therefore the people shun you like the plague."

Angrier than ever, the "reactionary and traditionalist parish priests" ask Jesus about his political position and about private property, capitalism, and the social question. Jesus answers:

> Do you want my real views? You are the vanguard of the exploiters. As someone has put it well, you do nothing but sell religious opium to narcotize the people and craze them so that they are no longer aware they are being oppressed. In the name of God, you preach resignation and submission to the powerful; you have thus broken God's commandment of love and have condemned the people to wretchedness, alienation from their true values, and death. What answer will you give at the judgment seat of history?

Woe to you, for you are more responsible than others, since you should be defenders of the law of love and brotherhood, but instead you have become sowers of hatred, and this in the name of God! How will you pay for this crime? You bless the rifles and machine guns of those who riddle the people with bullets, and you call holy the crimes of the exploiters.

On page 83 we are told that Jesus was killed by a burst from a machine gun, and he is buried with a machine gun in his hands to insinuate that he committed suicide.

On the last page comes the "resurrection": the people run into the streets "proclaiming that Jesus, the liberator, lives in the people and in the hearts of all who love social justice and seek liberation." (The word "liberation" and its derivatives occur 348 times in 78 pages, that is, an average of almost five times a page.)

When confronted with this example of "rereading," which a misuse of words calls a "Latin American reading of the Gospel," one asks whether the original text is approached with even a minimum of serious attention and respect.

The Bible is not to be read in either a materialist or a Latin American manner; rather, "the interpreter of sacred Scripture . . . should carefully investigate what meaning the sacred writers really intended, and what God wanted to manifest by means of their words" (*DV*, 12a/120). Unless we follow this basic and absolutely necessary rule, we slide into a situationalism and subjectivism that defy all controls and limits. The results will be as fanciful and grotesque as those of Everardo Ramírez Toro, former priest and former professor of theology.

No one will deny that any human situation — poverty or comfort, sickness or health, sadness or joy, captivity or freedom — can and should make us read the word of God with new eyes. The Gospel contains "all saving truth" (*DV*, 7a/115) and therefore always has a message for us. In its document on the unity of the faith and theological pluralism (1972), the International

Theological Commission says some excellent things in its ninth thesis:

> Because of the universality and missionary character of the Christian faith, it will always be necessary to rethink, reformulate, and re-experience the events and words revealed by God within each human culture, if we want to give a valid answer to the problems that deeply affect every human heart and are central to the prayer, worship, and daily life of the people of God. The Gospel of Christ thus brings every culture to its fulfillment, but also subjects it to creative criticism. As the local churches, under the direction of their bishops, undertake this difficult task of incarnating the Christian faith, they must ever preserve continuity and communion with the universal Church, past and present. Their efforts will contribute to the deepening of Christian life and the advancement of theological reflection within the universal Church, and will lead the human race, amid all its diversity, to the unity God wants for it.

6. Reappropriation of the Liturgy

In addition to taking to themselves the responsibility for directing their action within the Church, the "new Christians" who have been liberated from bourgeois ideology want "to reappropriate the liturgical and sacramental symbols and to strike out on new paths of contemplation, celebration, and Eucharist that will represent fidelity both to Christ and to the struggle of the poor for liberation." Thus no. 25 of the final statement issued by Christians for Socialism at Quebec.

The Second Commission of that convention offered this explanation:

> Political praxis is generating new values such as solidarity, hope, joy, courage, and so on, as well as a new sensibility that encourages

> us to celebrate our political commitment to the full. This "celebration of our history" of joint struggle is the first step toward a new liturgy, thanksgiving, and spiritual communion that have a real basis in political action but also transcend this action. This kind of liturgy, the form of which will depend on the creativity shown by Christians, is very difficult from any cyclical, historical liturgy, for it is the celebration of our surrender to God in historical events. This first appropriation of the emancipatory values that arise out of the new class praxis is the basis for the new experience and Christian symbolization proper to a Church of the People [16/ no. 2.4].

At the National Chilean Workshop of November 1972, the participants called attention to

> the urgent task of creating new liturgical forms that reflect a revolutionary commitment and give expression to the values found in the political struggles and political organizations of the people. The Eucharist, therefore, is not to be found in formulas and rubrics, but must be the living expression of a people that are fighting together against their oppressors. In this way a new spirituality will take shape that will be permanently related to the revolutionary commitment and to an ever new and surprising encounter with Christ the liberator [10/p. 257].

God alone knows what else the Christians for Socialism will invent in the name of the people and creativity — and, of course, the praxis of liberation — as they seek this unauthorized reappropriation of the liturgy. The Columbian episcopate, in a statement on these movements in its country (Nov. 21, 1976), said that

> the instrumentalization of the liturgy is perhaps the worst of their abuses. For them, the Eucharist has ceased to be the sacrifice and banquet of the Lord and has degenerated into a means of "consciousness raising," an instrument of the revolutionary struggle, an occasion for political harangues. Nothing restrains them, therefore, from scoffing at all the norms governing the celebration and

making up whatever prayers, formularies, and chants they please, from destroying the sacred meaning of the liturgy and turning it into an act of protest and an invitation to rebellion. A Eucharist thus profaned does not form a community of brothers but only incites a rally of comrades.[50]

In 1976 the Office of Educational Research and Action at Bogotá published *Prayer Based on the Praxis of Liberation*[51] as a book of prayers for those who have made a "class option" and chosen a type of "liberative praxis" that claims to find in revolution and the class struggle the only way to achieve full human liberation. The preface says: "You will not find here the abstract language of traditional documents or stereotyped sermons, nor the routine babbling of affected words and idealist language which marks so many liturgical prayers." These "prayers" are filled with criticisms of the Church, of orthodoxy and theology, and of what they reject as a "disincarnate theology." Those who use this book must see enemies everywhere and must cultivate hatred to such an extent that one is forced to ask how "Christians" could go to such extremes. Even the twenty-four eucharistic prayers are bathed in this atmosphere of conflict and hatred, which is called, by a misuse of words, a "praxis of liberation."

For example, the eucharistic prayer of the "Church of the poor" reads: "Let us pray for a Church that is poor and of the poor, a Church free . . . of structures." "Free us, Father, from our doctrinal and juridical securities. Make us true radicals when we proclaim your Gospel. . . . Free our pastors, too, from all ready-made responses . . . and from every concordat."

The eucharistic prayer "of the pilgrim Church" reads as follows:

> We ask your pardon because even in our time your Church continues to do violence to men's consciences. Even today we must deplore the authoritarian government, the pressures brought to bear and the threats used, the connivance with those in power who oppress the people, the lack of evangelical courage, the constant organizational and juridical subterfuges that prevent the one deci-

sive choice from ever being made: the choice of being a poor Church that is present in the lives of the poor. Help us all — bishops, priests, and laity — to be worthy of him who came only to serve and who imposed neither false obligations nor false certainties.

The eucharistic prayer "of pilgrim mankind": "Help us, Father, to keep the Church from her traditional preoccupations with doctrinal orthodoxy and the danger of heresy and obedience to authority."

The eucharistic prayer titled "The God Who Never Lets Us Settle Down":

> Father, hear our prayer for all those who have turned the Church into a place of soporific worship; for all those whose pious practices, ritual observances, and disquisitions on God have never inspired them to change their ways or commit themselves to the poor . . . ; for all those who have let themselves be lulled to sleep in the arms of the sacred, who stand for a soporific Christianity and are incapable of cursing the rich. . . . Help us to see you where you truly are, even today: tortured and harassed by the powerful. Help us to see and understand and to let ourselves be evangelized by the poor.

So it goes. We see again, this time in the form of "prayers," how this monotonous little world is turned in upon itself, how stultifying it is in its reduction of everything to a handful of slogans. The same worn phrases, the same terminology, the same directions keep reappearing, along with the same hatred of everything that is not egalitarian in the socialist manner, and the same hallucinations that cause these people to see ideology everywhere. At every point the same coldness toward the Church breaks through, the same ill will toward orthodoxy, the same contempt for doctrine, the same dislike of theologians, the same aversion from structures, the same antipathy to authority.

7. The Option for Marxist Socialism

The choice of socialism is basic and all determining. It explains the efforts, meetings, movements, struggles, sufferings, and sacrifices of those who seek to establish a "Church of the People." This is self-evidently the case with Christians for Socialism, as the very name indicates. Other related movements, however, also proclaim the necessity of this option and generally make it an indispensable condition for being "authentically" Christian. There is no point in providing extensive documentation of this fact; it will be enough to cite the joint statement by the Latin American Priests' Movements at its meeting in Lima:

> A comprehensive socialist option marks all of our Movements, as does the conviction that the revolutionary process in Latin America is leading to a socialist society. . . . Everyone acknowledges the importance of Marxism in the political and cultural world of Latin America. In this matter, our Movements recognize the contribution of Marxism, insofar as the latter aims at a scientifically rational history, connected with a praxis that constructively transforms the project of a new and different society [14/I.C].

The statement admits that Marxism in its present form presents problems and difficulties, especially "for a certain type of metaphysics." Consequently, the authors say, "it must be made clear that our Movements present nuances, and even divergences, in their evaluation of Marxism."

Not all of the movements are so cautious in their option for Marxism. The Fifth Commission of the International Convention said at Quebec: "A discernment exercised upon the options available, as well as the basic direction of the popular movement, have forced us, therefore, to choose a Marxist analysis of reality that is in harmony with our class option, and serves as a support and a guide to action" (29/3.2). The First Commission of the convention felt some scruples when it observed that some Christians "seem to lose their faith when they adopt Marxism" (25/5.3).

But "the problem of Christians who adopt Marxism and come in conflict with their faith causes us to ask what kind of Marxism they adopted. A consistent Marxist materialism need not necessarily include a metaphysics. But even if it does, the living God of the Christian faith does not belong in the world of metaphysics" (25/5.5).

What if it were possible to be, at the same time, a Christian and "an atheist in metaphysics"! The result would be something along the lines of what has occurred in Cuba, according to the Cuban report to the First Latin American Convention of Christians for Socialism: "We try to help them [the active, militant faithful] reach the liberating conclusion that a sincere Christian must be as much of an 'atheist' — in the Marxist sense — as any atheist is."[52]

In their Avila document, Christians for Socialism (CfS) call themselves, without qualification, "Marxist militants," and assert that "the choice of Marxist socialism, despite all the fears of the institutional Church, is for us, as twentieth-century Christians, a necessity that is consistent with our class option and our evangelical faith" (16/no. 52). Another Spanish document says that "when Christians for Socialism speak of a 'Marxist option,' they do not mean that they turn into Marxists on impulse, but that in the Marxist explanation of reality they find an accurate explanation of their own experience." And again: "At the end of this development of our faith we accept Marxism as a theory and a praxis that are indispensable if our Christian love is to take concrete form" (20/no. 42).

The same views are expressed by Christians for Socialism of Portugal (15/no. 3c–d) and Puerto Rico (31/p. 38).

This assured socialist or Marxist option results from a false dilemma. Christians for Socialism believes that there are only two choices: capitalism or socialism. "The growing acuteness of the class struggle makes it clear that there are only two possible alternatives in Latin America today: dependent capitalism with its resultant underdevelopment, or socialism" (4/I.1.13).[53]

Any attempt at a third solution is rejected as "third-wayism" or "reformism." These are the two charges constantly hurled at the Church's social teaching, which Christians for Socialism is unanimous in rejecting (see 7/pp. 424–30, the section on confrontation with "Christian reformism").

"We reject any effort to create 'Christian' political alternatives to capitalism and socialism" (31/p. 38), for the social teaching of the Church is "a pseudo-Christian ideology in the service of the [dominant] classes" (20/no. 49). The Second Commission at Quebec said the same thing: "Especially must we denounce the 'social teaching of the Church' as an instrument which the ruling class uses to keep its power" (26/5.3). In this area, Christians for Socialism will allow no consideration of other alternatives, no pluralism, no dialogue: "We wish to reject uncompromisingly the claim, widespread even in Christian circles, that Christians have a specific social plan, known as 'the social teaching of the Church.' We regard as a delusion the claim that the Gospel will, in the name of the primacy of the spiritual, point to any specific political platform" (22/p. 335).

It is a fact, however, that all who do not want to be regarded simply as Marxists "in the usual sense" (cf. 18/B.3) or as declared atheists must, willy-nilly, consider themselves "reformists," although of the left, not the right. They stand, in reality, for a Marxist reformism or a reformed and demetaphysicized Marxism.[54] It is very unlikely that the official versions of Marxism that now hold sway will accept a Marxism reformed or revised by priests and other Christians. The real Marxists, of course, will welcome the reformers and revisionists as stupid but useful people who can serve a purpose until the "dictatorship of the proletariat" is installed.

III. Conclusions

In this final section of our report we shall offer some conclusions, critical reflections, and theological guidelines that can be of help in our effort to be faithful to the Lord and his body the Church. We meet with denials and charges on every side; perplexity, doubt, and confusion are being sown and propagated even within the Church, with the explicit intention of causing doubt and hesitation. The goal of all these efforts is what is euphemistically called "a reformulation of the faith." In simple fact, the "reformulation" is nothing but a transformation of the very substance of the faith or its outright denial.

1. The "Church of the People" Is a New Sect

The "Church of the People" that is being proposed to us as an alternative type of ecclesial life is not our holy Catholic Church. It retains nothing of what the Second Vatican Council calls "the mystery of the Church," by which the Council means the Church is a divine, transcendent, saving reality which is present among men as

> both human and divine, visible yet invisibly endowed, eager to act yet devoted to contemplation, present in this world and yet not at home in it. She is all these things in such a way that in her

> the human is directed and subordinated to the divine, the visible likewise to the invisible, action to contemplation, and this present world to that city yet to come, which we seek [SC, 2/137–38].

This complex divine–human reality is comparable to the Incarnate Word himself; in it the human, earthly, visible, juridical, hierarchical, and social or institutional part is the organ or instrument which the Spirit of Christ uses in sanctifying and saving men (*LG,* 8a). In this context, moreover, salvation or liberation does not mean

> a purely immanent salvation, measured by material or even spiritual needs which relate solely to man's temporal existence and can be wholly identified with his temporal desires, hopes, occupations and struggles. No, it is a salvation which reaches far beyond these limited concerns and involves a communion with the sole Absolute, that is, with God. The salvation God offers us in Christ is, therefore, transcendent and eschatological; while it begins in this life, its culmination is in eternity.[55]

In the concept of the "Church of the People," which is offered to us as a new ecclesiology, we find nothing of all this, which is the very nature of Christ's body, constitutes its greatness, and elicits both our love for the Church and our commitment to her and her mission. The Chilean bishops, who experienced at firsthand the rise of this new and untraditional view of the Church, had this to say in their declaration of October 16, 1973, "Christian Faith and Political Activity" (no. 74):

> Hence it is not surprising that they [Christians for Socialism] detract from the nature of the Church and her essential institutionality. This leads to a "new Church," without a supernatural dimension, a hierarchical ministry, or sacraments. We cannot see this image as a simple "renovation" of the perennial Church. It is simply a different institution with different roots, means, and aims. It is, in short, a new sect. The fact is that the practical actions of

this group come dangerously close to being just that, more markedly as time goes on.[56]

There is no doubt that the Church should be "popular" or "of and for the people," and that it is, as Vatican II said, the people of God of the new covenant. The Council, however, understood by "people" not exclusively the poor and oppressed who have had their consciousness raised, but "all men" (*LG,* 13d/32): "All men are called to belong to the new People of God" (*LG,* 13a/30). However, although all men are called to the all-embracing unity of the people of God, not all in fact become members of this people. From the standpoint of actual belonging, Vatican II divided mankind into three categories (cf. *LG,* 13e): those who belong to the people of God in the full sense (Catholics; cf. *LG,* 14); those who incompletely or imperfectly but really belong to the people of God (baptized non-Catholic Christians, who possess in varying measure a variety of the elements constitutive of the Church) (cf. *LG*, 15; *UR*, 3b); and those who, without in the proper sense belonging to the people of God, are ordered to it in various ways (cf. *LG,* 16).

Vatican II thus uses the word "people" (of God) in a limited or stricter sense as meaning all those who are "fully" incorporated into the Church of Christ. In this sense, the "people of God" are all those who,

> possessing the Spirit of Christ, accept her entire system and all the means of salvation given to her, and through union with her visible structure are joined to Christ, who rules her through the Supreme Pontiff and the bishops. This joining is effected by the bonds of professed faith, of the sacraments, of ecclesiastical government, and of communion [*LG*, 14b/33].

It is easy to see, however, that while "people," thus understood, is restricttive and does not embrace all men, it has nothing to do with sociological distinctions between the poor and the rich, the governed and the governing, and so forth. Rich and poor alike, without distinction of social class, are a "people" and constitute the people of God of the new covenant, provided they satisfy the conditions indicated above. It is perfectly clear, on the other hand, that real oppressors, who practice injustice, do not satisfy those conditions: "He is not saved, however, who, though he is part of the body of the Church, does not persevere in charity. He remains indeed in the bosom of the Church, but, as it were, only in a 'bodily' manner and not 'in his heart' " (*LG,* 14b/33).

The Church thus described is the *true* Church of the people.

As long as we do not simplistically identify "people" and "poor," and as long as we understand the expression "people of God" as Vatican II understands it (it is a serious error in perspective, and utterly contrary to the Council, to identify the people of God solely with the laity), it is quite legitimate to say that the people of God are the bearer of the Gospel, constitute the Church, and have other privileges and prerogatives. We must never forget, however, that this Church of Christ is a priestly and prophetic community with an "organic structure" (*LG,* 11a/27). In it, all do not have the same functions, tasks, responsibilities, capacities, and competences; instead, there is a diversity of gifts, ministries, and works (cf. 1 Cor 12:4–6). Not everything is given to us by the sacrament of baptism, nor do we all receive the sacrament of orders.

2. A Terrible Dilemma

"We will not be won over" was one of the slogans at the Quebec convention (29/no. 4). The choice made by Christians for Socialism is unconditional: there is no disposition to engage in dialogue, no openness to possible correction. They assert that they are not to be won over but are stubbornly committed, without qualification, to the course they have undertaken. It is useless to talk to them in an effort to change them. If they take part in a meeting or course, they take the floor in season and out of season to repeat their commonplaces over and over and to reject any criticism of their views, no matter how profound it may be and how peaceably it may be offered. Anyone who does not think as they do is a "rightist," a "procapitalist," an "ideologue," a "fascist." "As for ourselves, we cannot live the faith in any other way, because to live it in any other way would mean, to our conscience, living it on the side, and as supporters, of the oppressors" (21/14.1). The dilemma is clear: "Either abandon Christianity or live it in a radically new way" (22/p. 336).

When confronted with these alternatives: Change your basic choice (of being a Christian) or change Christianity, many of the Christians for Socialism are perfectly sure of their course. They must turn Christianity into something new. They will not adapt to the Church; the Church must adapt to them.

It is easy to understand how a Christian, sincerely committed to this kind of ideological and revolutionary struggle, does not feel at home in the Church. The contradictions are too evident. He has lost his love for the institutional Church, and no other Church exists to take its place. This is why the idea of abandoning the Church or breaking with her seems to be a widespread and constant temptation in these groups, and to many it brings real suffering. The various slogans — "We will not be forced into isolation" (29/no. 4); "We will not be won over" (ibid.); "There must be an ideological debate within the Church" (15/4.a); "Class struggle within the institutional Church!" (27/1.2); "Struggle within the Church!" (21/no. 25); "Keep up the ideological struggle with the hierarchy" (30/4.1), and do so "as priests" or "because we are priests" (14/I.3) — express the various reasons why these people remain and wish to remain in the Church. Such reasons, however, are purely strategic and external and, to that extent, insincere; and because they are insincere, they are neither sufficient nor satisfactory. The result is suffering.

Pablo Richard, a Chilean and a former priest, describes the "terrible dilemma" in these words:

When the class struggle and the confrontation with the bourgeois bloc become acute, priests are faced with the terrible dilemma of a "double fidelity": fidelity, on the one hand, to the people and their struggles, and fidelity, on the other, to a hierarchical Church that is becoming daily more fully allied to the ruling bloc. This dilemma makes some priests waver; others it makes back down or at least undermines their ideological clarity or political combativeness.[57]

François Houtart, a Belgian canon, well known in Latin America for his sociological researches, recently issued a statement that describes the dilemma and situation in the Church of many of his fellow priests:

> I think of the Church as not only an oppressive institution but also a community of men who share my faith and without whom I cannot live that faith. I cherish the hope that I can change the Church from within, not by confronting the hierarchy directly, but by endeavoring to change things from the bottom up. Of course, if a conflict were inevitable and if a critical adherence to the institution were no longer possible, my options as a Christian and a socialist would be clear; these would include even a break with the Church.[58]

"A break with the Church." There is the dilemma inevitably caused by the inner dynamism of Christians for Socialism and the related movements we have been studying. Their "alternative ecclesial life" is already, in fact, a break with the Church.

3. Division within the Church

The documentation on which the present study is based should open our eyes and enable us to see clearly that the seeds of a major internal division are already present in our Catholic Church.

The movements we have been studying are determined not to leave the Church but to remain and promote the ideological struggle within her bosom. They consider this their primary task. *Cromos,* a journal published in Bogotá, reported in its issue of June 9, 1976, that ten groups of priests who were in "defiance" of the Church hierarchy had broken their silence to "clarify their positions," but "were maintaining their incognito as part of their political tactics in dealing with the bishops." They explained: "The Catholic Church in Colombia is divided into two great groups, and the division is becoming daily more marked. There is the Church that is on the side of the exploiters, and there is the Church that is on the side of the oppressed." Of the latter they say:

> What we have is not a homogeneous group but a broad trend, the basis of which is a commitment to those who are suffering or who are experiencing hunger, nakedness, the lack of tools for work and the means of production, and so forth. In terms of organization, this Church is represented by at least fifty groups that are national in scope, while in each diocese, each community, each school directed by religious, and in each parish with several priests, there exist groups which share this broad trend.

Although such talk is sometimes exaggerated, there is no doubt that a division of the Church "into two great groups" seems to be the most serious internal problem of the Church in Latin America. It is clearly not in accord with the facts to characterize the two groups as the above-quoted passage does, that is, with one group on the side of the "exploiters" and the other on the side of the "oppressed," as though the basis of the division were social. To see the situation in these terms is to fall into the simplism that divides mankind into only two classes: the oppressors and the oppressed.

As a matter of fact, however, the cause — and it is indeed a serious one — of the present division of the Church into two groups is a divergence in concepts of the Church and in the ecclesiologies that lie behind these concepts. On one side we have those who accept the Catholic Church as she defines herself in the documents of Vatican II, with her hierarchy, her magisterium, and the whole "institutional" dimension that is of divine origin. (It is contrary to the facts to assert that this Church is not also, and even prefers to be, at the side of the poor and the oppressed.) On the other side we have those who reject this one and only Church and look eagerly for a "new Church," a utopian "Church of the People."

4. Instrumentalization of the Church

The constant charges that the Church has "ideologized" the faith; the effort to "liberate" the consciences of the masses by introducing qualitative changes in Christian morality; the "reinterpretation" of the faith (which is reduced in the end to a simple political act) by denying or transforming the very content of the Catholic faith; the capricious (materialist) "rereading" of the Bible; the arbitrariness that marks the so-called reappropriation of the liturgy by the people; the choice of Marxist socialism, with all that this entails of hatred and class conflict; all this should lead logically to the abandonment of the Catholic Church or a break with her. Nevertheless, as we have seen, Christians for Socialism assert their right to remain in the Church and to set up within her, and in opposition to her, their new ecclesial alternative, the "Church of the People."

From the various statements of Christians for Socialism, we know, however, that it is not out of love for the Church, much less in order to be identified with her, that its members hold their places within her. They remain in order to play the role of a Trojan horse and carry on their ideological struggle within her ranks (cf. 21/no. 38).

With this as their declared goal, they seek also to continue in the priestly ministry. This retention of the priesthood for tactical reasons was made evident at the very beginning of the Christians for Socialism movement. Pablo Richard says as much: "As a beginning, we deliberately seek to form a movement *of priests*. . . . We emphasize this priestly character of the movement because for the masses in city and countryside the priest is the spiritual and ideological leader in his milieu. At the public and social level, too, the sociological role of the priest is decisive."[59]

This was written about Chile, 1971, the period that saw the coming on the scene of "the Eighty" (priests), "the Two Hundred" (priests), the Secretariat for Priests of the Christians for Socialism, the letter of the twelve professors of theology at the Catholic University of Chile, and the presentation for a First Latin American Convention. Even the letter of invitation to this convention showed a preoccupation with "the 'tactical' use of Christianity, and the cultural role of the priest in our society."[60]

When Gonzalo Arroyo S.J., secretary general of Christians for Socialism, analyzed the Latin American situation in 1972, he saw that to the masses the Church was the voice of Christianity. Concretely, this meant that the bishops and priests speak for Christianity. "Consequently, from a sociological standpoint, a break with the present Church, even though she is so often committed to the privileged, would surely be on the whole politically ineffective, since it would greatly restrict our sphere of action" (8/p. 387).

The main reason, then, for not breaking with the Church and for asserting the right to remain in her, even as priests, is "the greater political effectiveness" they will have in these circumstances. Arroyo cites the example of the Golconda group in Colombia: "They began by denouncing the hierarchy and obsessively attacking everything that Cardinal Concha and others did." What was the result? "This led to the suspension of the priests, their removal from their parishes, and their being forced to become taxi drivers or something similar; in the end, their influence was almost completely destroyed." Arroyo cites another example, the Young Church movement in Chile, which attacked the hierarchy and thereby lost its effectiveness. "We have learned from this and drawn conclusions from their experience. It is not appropriate to move along those lines, even though some would like to in order to differentiate themselves clearly from a Church they regard as a Church of the rich and the powerful. From their viewpoint, this course may be manly, but it would greatly limit our field of action."

Such, then, is the reason why they wish to remain in the Church.

> The fact that a large number of priests belong to our movement gives it a symbolic force and enables it to carry a much greater symbolic weight with many Christians than if the priests were not members. For the moment, then, the presence of so many priests is useful for reaching the Christian masses whose consciousness has not yet been raised and who are not yet politicized. It increases and intensifies the effectiveness of our quest for socialism [8/p. 391].

The Latin American Priests' Movements, which formed a federation at a meeting in Lima in February 1973, are aware of how worthwhile this political strategy is. "Our status as priests adds a special dimension to our revolutionary commitment. In the Latin American world, in which the Church — the institutional Church — plays an important political role, our membership in her as priests gives us a place in society, a special authority, possibilities of effective action, and specific roles which we must assume" (14/no. 3).

> It is important to emphasize that, *as a movement of priests,* our political role is real and quite special, insofar as we exercise a priestly activity, that is, insofar as we exercise our priesthood within the Church and in solidarity with the popular classes. This will allow us to act as evangelizers and to enjoy a position as priests

in Christian communities that are living their faith in the form of a political commitment [no. 4].

Priests for Latin America (SAL) adopted the same strategy in its "Minimal Consensus," in which it states this resolution: "We see it as a basic choice that our commitment to the oppressed should be *as priests;* our own vocation, and the people themselves, require this of us. We must therefore have a priestly identity, and this, in the present circumstances, requires a theological restatement of what the priesthood is."[61] In other words, the theology of the ordained ministry must be changed.

In their own minds and hearts, these men consider themselves to be without ties to the Church. They do not attribute the slightest importance to the statements of the pope or the orders of the bishops. They even publicly oppose the norms and directives issued by those in authority, and they do not stop short of rejecting the authoritative teachings of the ecumenical councils. They attempt to organize and live "an alternative type of ecclesial life" and to carry on "the ideological struggle with the hierarchy" with the help of "base communities" that are not ecclesial in character or are even utterly outside the Catholic communion. Nonetheless, these same men claim the right to exercise their priestly ministry, despite the fact that "since the priestly ministry is the ministry of the Church herself, it can be discharged only by hierarchical communion with the whole body" (*PO,* 15c/564).

5. A False Concept of Evangelization

In the documents we have been studying is a concept that has evident consequences for our whole mission and pastoral life, especially in catechetics. We refer to the concept that Christians for Socialism has of evangelization, and one example will suffice.

The First Commission of the Quebec convention says that the

poor "are the ones who build the Church" and that "for this reason we reject the manipulative practice of going out and evangelizing the people as though we were the proprietors of the truth. The people are evangelized when they begin to evangelize themselves" (25/2.7). It seems, then, that the solemn charge, "Go, therefore, and teach," does not apply any more! But no good evangelizer has ever thought of himself as the proprietor of the truth; rather, he is entrusted with it, he has inherited it, he is the servant of a truth he received and is happy to pass to others.

Today all this must change. If we want to "go and evangelize the people," the only thing we have to bring them are the tools of Marxism! This manner of conceiving evangelization is evidently connected closely with what we said earlier about "faith" as a political, revolutionary, and liberating act; about "revelation" in and through the ongoing history the people are shaping; about the people who are identified with the poor and oppressed, who have their "consciousness raised," and who, it is said, are the sole agent even of theology; about the alleged prophetic, missionary, and epistemological privileges of the poor; and, above all, about the concept of praxis, which is identified with the revolutionary struggle for "liberation," which in turn is identified with "evangelization" ("the people are automatically Christian when they are struggling for their liberation").

6. Subversion

We Christians of Latin America frequently find ourselves in quite difficult situations; this is true of almost all the countries of the continent. It is undeniable that there are injustices, sinful situations, and, as the Medellín statement on peace pointed out (no. 16), institutionalized violence. It is part of our evangelizing mission to denounce these situations and fight against them. Many episcopal conferences have in recent years attempted to meet this serious obligation. It can be said that in not a few Latin American republics, ruled as they are in almost every case by military governments which follow the very questionable doctrine that national security is more important than personal security, the Church (and specifically the hierarchy, i.e., the bishops and priests) is still the only power that can make a prophetic voice heard and can say, like John the Baptist, "It is not right for you to . . ." (Mk 6:19).

As a result, not a few of these ecclesiastics are accused of being "subversives," "Marxists," and "Communists" and are subjected to terrible persecution, violence, torture, and even death. We live in an age of witnesses ("confessors," as they were called in an earlier time) and martyrs. We were not all prepared for a calling so difficult and yet so evangelical: "Blest are you when they insult you and persecute you and utter every kind of slander against you because of me. Be glad and rejoice, for your reward is great in heaven; they persecuted the prophets before you in the very same way" (Mt 5:11–12).

If this be subversion, then subversive we must be. In a courageous "Pastoral Charge to the People of God" (Oct. 25, 1976), the Commission of Representatives of the National Conference of Brazilian Bishops said: "The injurious and iniquitous activity, carried on anonymously and publicly, of those who charge bishops, priests, and laity with being subversives, agitators, and communists, whenever they go to the defense of the poor, the lowly, the prisoner, and the victim of torture, is contributing to the climate and practice of violence and outrage."

Those who courageously and authoritatively issue such reproofs, and who take action against the scorners of human rights,[62] are not to be compared, in ideas, motivations, and methods, with Christians for Socialism and others who are striving to establish a heretical Church of the People. It is not necessary, in order to oppose injustice, that we make a "class option" of the socialist-Marxist type or foster the struggle of one social class against the other. In a study of the Marxist and Christian concepts of social conflict, Pierre Bigo S.J. speaks with magisterial clarity and prudence:

> We can thus see how great the differences are between Christianity and Marxism when it comes to the class struggle. We might say with greater accuracy: the differences between thinking that acknowledges all human rights (such thinking is not confessional, for its focus is simply on man as such) and thinking that is inspired by dialectical materialism.
>
> According to the first type of thinking, the goal of the class struggle is not the abolition of the class of independent workers, but the elimination of injustice from the relations between investor and salaried worker, or, more broadly, the elimination of unearned profit. This implies a very definite concept of social class.
>
> The social class that must be eliminated is, in the Christian view, the class that profits from rewards disproportionate to the service rendered or from a surplus value that corresponds to no service at all. In other words, what must be eliminated is property insofar as it is the source of *privileges,* in the strict sense of this last term. A privilege is every profit that is unearned or is earned unjustly. It is also property insofar as it is the fruit and cause of a corresponding *power* in society, a power that uses every means at its disposal (corruption, direct interference in the political sphere, the mass media) to maintain the source of its privileges.
>
> If a social class is defined by these illegitimate *privileges* and *powers,* it is a social class that should be abolished. *In this sense,* it can be said that a Christian works toward a classless society in which one sector of the population cannot secure the necessities of life by means which are not at the disposal of all, or in which one part of the population is unwilling to participate on the same conditions as others.[63]

The statement on peace issued by the Second General Conference of the Latin American Episcopate (Medellín, 1968) makes it clear that not every form of wretchedness is the result of a sinful situation, since "at times the misery in our countries can have natural causes which are difficult to overcome."[64] The bishops do not overlook the positive efforts being made at various levels to build a more just society. Nor do they condemn all forms of inequality among men, but only those that are excessive or unjust.[65]

In our efforts to promote justice, we must bear in mind that not every social inequality is automatically unjust. All men are indeed fundamentally equal, "since all men possess a rational soul and are created in God's likeness, since they have the same nature and origin, have been redeemed by Christ, and enjoy the same divine calling and destiny" (*GS,* 29a/227). On the other hand, "all men are not alike from the point of view of varying physical power and the diversity of intellectual and moral resources" (*GS,* 29b/227). Consequently, "rightful differences exist between men" (*GS,* 29c/228).

Given the difficulties the Church is having with many Latin American governments, it is important to clarify the concept of subversion. It is a key concept in the present situation, but its use is marked by ambiguities that must be brought to light.

The documents we have been studying repeatedly insist on the necessity of the "class struggle," in the Marxist sense of the words. We have also seen that their "socialist option" tends in fact to be a Marxist option. There is no point in repeating the many citations; the texts and contexts are quite clear. We shall simply offer one further example, from the synthesis of the work of the commissions and the main lines of the National Chilean Workshop sponsored by Christians for Socialism in November 1972. According to this statement, Christians for Socialism "adopt the Marxist analysis as their own and make it their immediate objective to collaborate in the takeover of power by the working class."[66]

This is indeed subversion. Those who speak in this way and try to act in accord with such an ideology can in all justice be accused of being subversives or Marxists. Subversion and Marxism, in the truest sense of the words, are exemplified in what Christians for Liberation said and resolved at its Second National Congress in Riobamba, Ecuador: the creation of a new man in a new society "is possible only if the proletariat takes political power, that is, if a dictatorship of the proletariat — which is authentic popular democracy — is established" (30/2.2).

For this reason, various Latin American governments are not always mistaken when they apply the terms "subversive" or "Marxist" to the language and proceedings of certain bishops, priests, and religious men and women. How can these colleagues in the ministry or the religious life be defended in the name of the Gospel message and the body of Christ, which is his Church? The struggle to enable the proletariat to take political power and establish their dictatorship is *not* evangelization and has nothing to do with the redemptive mission of Jesus Christ and the pastoral task of the Church. It is subversion pure and simple: against the state and against the Church.

7. The "Remnant of Medellin"?

Christians for Socialism and related movements or groups — all of them made up of leftist Christians — delight in claiming to be the only ones who are truly faithful to the teachings and statements of the Second General Conference of the Latin American Episcopate (1968), as expressed in the Medellín documents. Thus the Spanish journal *Vida Nueva* (no. 1020 [Mar. 5, 1976], pp. 28–29) suggests that the "remnant of Medellín" is now to be found in such revolutionary groups as ONIS, SAL, CfS, etc. Everyone else — episcopal conferences, pastoral institutes, and especially the Latin American Episcopal Conference (CELAM) since its Fourteenth Regular Meeting at Sucre, Bolivia, in November 1972 — is accused of infidelity to the Medellín documents and of turning to the right. The charge is in accord, of course, with the view of those who see only two possible choices: the left or the right. All who do not turn to the left, by making a class and socialist (Marxist) option in behalf of the poor (all of whom by the fact of their poverty are also "oppressed"), necessarily belong to the right and are in favor of the "oppressors" (since all the non-poor, i.e., those who have found some fulfillment in life, are "exploiters"). These "rightists" have a "bourgeois," "ideologized" faith, etc., etc. Since, furthermore, the Medellín documents are, in their view, leftist, they can triumphantly parade themselves as the loyal "remnant of Medellín."

However, we shall look in vain to the Medellín documents for the choices and positions which characterize and identify these various movements. There is in the Medellín documents not a single text that shows a choice of Marxist socialism, that betrays a class option or an option exclusively of the poor and against the rich, that makes such an option an indispensable condition of attaining the truth, or that says all the poor are oppressed and all others are oppressors. There is not a single text that declares that only the oppressed who have had their consciousness raised by Marxist methods are the locus of encounter with God, sole bearer of the authentic Gospel, true subjects of the Church, and exclusive possessors in the Church of epistemological, missionary, and prophetic privileges. Not a single texts says that the revolutionary praxis of liberation is the necessary starting point for a genuine understanding of faith and theology, or that such a praxis is source, norm, and judge of truth. Not a single text acknowledges the ongoing history of the Latin American peoples to be the locus of the constitutive divine revelation on which our faith is based. Not a single text requires a radical deideologization of the inherited faith, on the grounds that in the past the Church did nothing but weaken, deform, adulterate, and betray the Gospel of Jesus Christ. Not a single texts rejects the social teaching of the Church as "third-wayism" or "reformism." And so on and so on.

Absolutely nothing of this kind can be found in the Medellín documents. The choices and positions therein stated, which in an admirable and providential manner open the way for the purification and renewal of the people of God in Latin America, are inspired and directed by an utterly different mentality and spirit: the mentality and spirit that guided the Second Vatican Council. The purpose of the Medellín meeting and the documents it produced was "to correct the course of the Church on the vast Latin American continent, in order to bring it into accord with the directives of Vatican II."[67]

8. The Liberation of Theology

One of the attributes assigned to the people made up of the poor and oppressed who have had their "consciousness raised" is that they are the "subject" of theology, that is, the "makers" of theology, the "theologians." (We have seen the texts that insist on this point.) Consequently, we find the promoters of the new "Church of the People" a widespread contempt for the professional theologians because the latter are not "committed to," much less "identified with," what the former call the people. This disdain for theologians brings with it contempt for their theology. The result is that the former neither has nor wants a good, solid, broad, reflective, and mature theology. In fact, they have no theology at all.

This is surely the reason why some "theologians of liberation" make a show of living with the people who are poor and oppressed, who have had their consciousness raised, and who are now involved in the "struggle." In the eyes of these men, this title is far more valuable than any academic title (which, in any case, they almost always lack). One of them who indeed possesses good academic credentials, Joseph Comblin, says: "I was a professor until 1958. Since then I have ceased to be one, and if I still am [*sic*], it is only in order to earn my living . . . I am no longer an academic theologian, because I am no longer capable of really teaching as they do in a European university."[68]

Here we have the "liberation" of theology. These men are no longer willing to be professors or to teach seriously, with the methodology, competence, and preparation required in the strict universities of the Old World. Such methods belong in banks. Everything now comes from the "people" and depends on the epistemological, missionary, and prophetic privileges of the "people." The people think, listen to the word, are not deceived, and do not sin. Above all, the people possess the authentic praxis, the only one that counts. The people are transformed into a legend. Anyone who makes a "class option," in favor of the one class and against the other, has the doors of truth thrown wide open to him, and study is no longer needed; he is the true, real theologian. Those who once studied the antiquated, "ideologized" theology now try to forget it so that they may be schooled by the people, who form the new magisterium. "Taking a course to be a deacon is a method proper to the oppressor."[69]

The true source of light is the praxis of liberation and revolution. On the basis of practice, and working with, in, and for praxis, men are now capable of offering a "new theology" in two pages, just as in a few lines they can reject a whole theology that is centuries old, simply, by labeling it "European." Perhaps this is why we are experiencing a horde of "theologies" in Latin America; but they are so superficial, and their claims so unserious and unscientific, that we gradually lose our capacity for astonishment as we read all the tomfoolery and nonsense.

All this explains Juan Luis Segundo's severe criticism of the theology of liberation.[70] He considers it to be "born of a pastoral situation," a concrete need: "that of giving a backing that was both theological and Christian to those who were committing themselves" (p. 93). It was thus a kind of "theology under pressure," a theology in a pastoral hurry. It seemed urgent to choose and act, without time for prior long-range theological and ideological reflection; choices had to be based on the system of see–judge–act. "I can remember countless meetings at which the whole emphasis was on 'seeing' and 'acting,' and precious little attention was given to 'judging' " (p. 96). "In these circumstances people ended up with a very partial knowledge of the Bible in this first 'theology under pressure' of liberation. In practice, the Bible was reduced not to the Gospels but to a few passages of the Old Testament that touched on the politics of the people of Israel."

Segundo complains that this hasty theology of liberation disregards the relative autonomy of theology, that is, that theology "cannot be done without respecting the rules proper to it; that theology must be taken more seriously as a science; that when done hastily and under pressure, it cannot be made to serve real needs; that its methods must be taken seriously, because they possess a relative autonomy and cannot be ignored" (p. 97). Therefore, "time and effort are required if [theology and thinking about the faith] are to be creative; if time and effort cannot be given to the task, it is much better to avoid theology" (pp. 100–101).

9. The "Theology of Liberation"

In the beginning, the theology of liberation was meant to be a local, Latin American theology, inspired by the concerns and directives of the Medellín documents. Gradually, however, Christians of the left turned it into a "tool" and made it "their" theology.

Gustavo Gutiérrez attended the meetings of Christians for Socialism from the beginnings of the movement in Chile[71] to the convention in Quebec; his *Theology of Liberation* was published in 1971, even before the official establishment of Christians for Socialism. Gonzalo Arroyo, secretary general of Christians for Socialism, reported in 1972 that "our entire theological formation has taken this turn [toward a faith that focuses on liberation] because of our contact with Gustavo Gutiérrez and other theologians" (8/p. 370).

Concerning that same period, Pablo Richard tells us that "in Chile the popular movement had its own rich theology, while it was in the Christians for Socialism movement that the 'theology of liberation' developed in a practical way that was meant for the masses."[72] The Puerto Rican Christians for Socialism says: "We identify with the Latin American theologians who have developed the 'theology of liberation.' This theology represents a critical reflection on the concrete historical praxis of liberation" (31/p. 37).

As a matter of fact, what is today widespread and goes under the name, in Latin America, of "theology of liberation" is a fanciful mixture of Christian ideals, socialist utopianism, and Marxist methods that inspires those leftist movements which, for tactical reasons, still call themselves Christian and dream of a "new Church" that differs from the Catholic Church. Christians for Socialism is one of the names the theology of liberation has taken. A document on "imperialist penetration of the Latin American Church" (written by Latin Americans exiled in Paris and presented in Rome at the January 1976 session of the Russell War Crimes Tribunal) speaks of the "theology of liberation" ("a specifically Latin American current of thought, the first that is independent of European theology") and says of it that "in Chile and several other countries this current produced a movement called 'Christians for Socialism,' which is made up of Christians who . . . reject the third-way solutions inspired by the 'social teaching of the Church.' "[73]

10. The Problem of Praxis

A chief preoccupation of this "new way of theologizing" is its eagerness for praxis or action, which represents a reaction against certain excessive forms of pure speculation. At any rate, Christians for Socialism wants an "orthopraxis," and its concern is certainly a "sign of the times" that must be recognized and in which we must try to discern God's will for us (cf. *GS*, 11a). The men of our day, especially the young, are increasingly sensitive to situations of injustice and, unfortunately, there are plenty of these situations. The past century was especially sensitive in matters of liberty; the present century has a sharpened sensibility in the area of justice, and this sensibility is profoundly Christian.

This sign of the times is accompanied by another: contemporary man feels an instinctive and growing distrust of any purely doctrinal message of liberation; he judges the value of such messages according to the basic criterion of their effectiveness in procuring real liberation; he asserts the primacy of praxis. Praxis and orthopraxis now provide the norm for evaluating doctrinal messages. Men believe in deeds rather than in doctrines. For this reason, effective commitment to liberation is an absolutely necessary proof of credibility for the Church in today's world. Unless the Church takes a special interest in liberation, unless she commits herself actively and effectively to this goal, she is not credible to modern man.

In a document which the Commission for Justice and Peace prepared for the Synod of Bishops in 1974, we read: "The present world situation as seen in the light of faith bids us return to the heart of the Christian message and convince ourselves of its true meaning and pressing demands. The mission of preaching the Gospel in our time requires that we commit ourselves to the full liberation of man even in his earthly life." As the synod of 1971 had observed, "unless the Christian message of love and justice shows its effectiveness through action in the cause of justice in the world, it will only with difficulty gain credibility with the men of our times."[74]

Recently Pope Paul VI, in his "Apostolic Exhortation on Evangelization," made the same point:

> People often claim these days that our age hungers for sincerity and authenticity. The young, especially, are said to abhor all that

is false and fictitious and to look only for the transparently true.

Such "signs of the times" bid us be on the alert. For, tacitly or aloud, they put implacable questions to us: Do you yourselves believe what you say? Do you live what you believe? Do you preach what you live? More than ever before, living witness is the necessary condition of fully effective preaching. Consequently, we must look to ourselves as responsible, to a degree, for all the success and efficacy of the Gospel we proclaim.[75]

We may not grant that praxis is the sole and unconditional criterion of truth, but we must indeed admit that, especially today, praxis is an indispensable criterion of credibility. Nonetheless, we would be denying the very problem of truth if we were to allow that what is not successful in terms of science or action is not true. To identify truth with praxis and to pass over all the problems raised by truths which no positive method can verify would be to fall into a new positivism. In its instruction on the theological formation of future priests (1976), the Sacred Congregation for Catholic Education notes that a theology of the word "cannot be replaced by a *theology of praxis,* which prescinds from any metaphysical commitment and reduces theology to the *human sciences* and, consequently, to a phenomenologism and pragmatism."[76]

We cannot turn theology into "praxology." We can indeed say, with the Second Vattican Council, that the word of God is "the saving Word" (*PO,* 4b/539); that Christian faith is our response to what God has willed to reveal "for the sake of our salvation" (*DV,* 11b/119); and that, consequently, the content of our faith is truths "of salvation" (*DV,* 7a/115) or "the source of all life for the Church" (*LG,* 20a/39). At the same time, however, we maintain that our Christian faith contains great truths of the speculative order which deserve much study, meditation, and contemplation; that is, we maintain (in the words of Vatican Council I) that "when reason, enlightened by faith, searches with diligence, devotion, and modesty, it attains with God's help to some understanding of the mysteries, an understanding that is extremely fruitful."[77]

This same diligent, pious, and modest reflection, meditation, and contemplation of the faith leads, by its very nature (since we are dealing with "truths of salvation"), to the practical living out of what we believe. The International Theological Commission, in the sixth thesis of its statement on the relations between the Church's magisterium and theology (1975), says: "The specifically theological authority of the theologians derives from the scientific status of their discipline. This status in turn, however, must reflect the special character of this science, which is a science of the faith and cannot be properly elaborated without a living experience and practice of the faith."

Christ himself alludes to this aspect of faith: "Any man who desires to come to me will hear my words and put them into practice" (Lk 6:47, cf. Mt 7:24). In Christ's use of the word, however, "practice" means "bearing fruit" (cf. Lk 6:43; cf. Mt 12:33–35) or "good works," that is, all that he asked or commanded and, above all, the love of God. Only the "faith which expresses itself through love" is our Christian faith.

For the true Christian who is trying to live his faith according to the demands of the Gospel and the teaching of the Church there is no such thing as a purely speculative faith or, as some would put it these days, no "orthodoxy" pure and simple. There is only a constant effort to put the faith into practice. In other words, there is praxis or orthopraxis. The possible opposition or tension between orthodoxy and orthopraxis is primarily a personal problem for the individual Christian. Christians have been aware of this ever since the day when St. James wrote:

> My brothers, what good is it to profess faith without practicing it? Such faith has no power to save one, has it? . . . Show me your faith without works, and I will show you the faith that underlies my works! Do you believe that God is one? You are quite right. The demons believe that, and shudder. Do you want proof,

you ignoramus, that without works faith is idle?" (Jm 2: 14, 18-20).

According to a "new way of theologizing" theology is a "reflection on praxis." The praxis in question is regarded, as we have seen, as "the theological source par excellence" and "the matrix that generates a new theological creativity," as "the point of departure for interpreting revelation" and "the horizon within which everything is to be seen," as "the organizing principle of theology" and "the source of truth," as the "sole locus of theological interpretation" and "the locus of truth," as "the Christian tribunal of final instance for judging the truth or falsity of the faith" and "the criterion of truth," as the "first moment in the interpretation and rereading of the Lord's word" and "the supreme norm of truth and value."

Despite the great importance given to praxis as source, criterion, and judge of truth and faith, those who speak of praxis in these terms make almost no effort to define praxis or to justify the epistemological positions taken. From a vague "Christian praxis" they pass easily to "historical praxis," from "historical praxis" to "social praxis," which is simply identified with "the praxis of liberation," and finally from "the praxis of liberation" to a "revolutionary praxis" which is meant to establish socialism. The praxis of which they speak or which they presuppose is "the action of man in history," "the transformation of the world," or, more concretely, "the socialist revolution that leads to liberation." In short, they mean praxis in the Marxist sense.

It is very easy to accept uncritically the Marxist concept of praxis and then to make of it the source of the Christian faith or a tribunal of final instance for judging the truth or falsity of the faith or the supreme norm of truth and value. However, there is nothing scientific about such a procedure, nor can it be taken seriously as theology. It represents a new way indeed of theologizing, but the new way is simply barbarous.

Theological concern for praxis is nothing new; it did not begin with Karl Marx. On the contrary, the desire to base theology on praxis has a long, seven-century-old tradition in Catholic theology. This tradition provides us with a concept of praxis that has been the object of systematic study and profound reflection. It holds that a theology without praxis is harmful. But in this case, praxis means the love of God as an elicited act of the will that is essentially posterior to intellection and conformed to intellection which proceeds correctly from a mind enlightened by revelation.[78]

11. A Single History?

The ideologues of the "Church of the People" regard monism in history to be a dogma beyond discussion. The reason they are so strong on the thesis of "a single history" is simple: if there is a single history, and if that history is a "history of salvation," then the poor and oppressed who have had their consciousness raised and are now liberators, and who must also create this one history, are likewise the creators of the history of salvation! The "historical actions" of the poor, etc., are also "salvific actions," and actions that build the Church! "The poor are the creators of both history and the Church" (25/2.7). Consequently, it would be dualism, in their view, to distinguish between Church and world. That is why they see and attack various "dualisms" in traditional theology, which is not "Latin American."

> There is but a single history that is liberating (that is, saving) and was set in motion by God at the moment of creation. It is the Spirit that guides this history both within the people of God and outside of it; but we can also say that in critical situations the Spirit prefers to manifest himself outside of the people of God. The important thing is not to be Christian but to liberate the oppressed, as the parable of the last judgment makes clear [5/p. 223].

Francisco Vanderhoff and Miguel Angel Campos write:

> The unity of human history is a basic theme of Latin American theology. This theology thus moves beyond the kind of antagonistic dualism that separates secular history (the history of temporal realities and political societies) from sacred history or the history of salvation, and identifies the latter with the history of Israel or the history of the Church. Latin American theology regards human history as the only history there is; everything in it is part of the history of salvation, and the latter is not to be reduced to the history of Israel or of the Church. This means that there can be no setting up of a dualism in which a so-called history of salvation (whether of Israel, or of the Church, or of anything else) is hierarchically superimposed on human history (which in fact is the only history there really is).[79]

In this, as in almost all the positions they take, the promoters of the "Church of the People" draw inspiration from "their" theologian, who is always at their side: Gustavo Gutiérrez. It must be said, however, that in his *Theology of Liberation* Gutiérrez is exaggeratedly optimistic about "the unequivocal assertion of the universality of salvation" (p. 152). He tells his readers that a revision in the way the problem of salvation is posed "has led to the clear and simple affirmation of the universality of salvation" (p. 179, n. 6). What is meant by this is not simply the universal salvific will of God, or that all men are called to communion with God, or that all men *can* be saved; what is meant is that all are *in fact* saved: "There is more to the idea of the universality of salvation than simply asserting the possibility of reaching it while outside the visible frontiers of the Church" (p. 151).

In other words, is there no possibility of eternal damnation? No hell? But is this really evident? Is it a doctrine that is "clear and simple" and "unequivocal"? The thesis that "history is one" (pp. 153–68) is based on the weak premise that salvation is in fact universal: "The idea of a universal salvation, which was accepted only with great difficulty and was based on the desire to expand the possibilities of achieving salvation, leads to the question of the intensity of the presence of the Lord and therefore of the religious significance of man's action in history" (p. 152).

There is another premise. Gutiérrez later seeks to persuade us that mankind — every individual — is the temple of God (pp. 190–94): "Furthermore, not only is the Christian a temple of God; every man is" (p. 193). This important and unqualified assertion is "proved" simply by the story of Cornelius (a fairly typical example of generalizing from an isolated instance). Gutiérrez then cites two texts, one of Congar, the other of St. Augustine, to the effect that "many" invisibly constitute the temple of God, and he then shifts without further ado from "many" to "all." This section ends with the statement that "since God has become man, humanity, every man, history, is the living temple of God. The 'pro-fane,' that which is located outside the temple, no longer exists" (p. 194). A new section, "Conversion to the Neighbor," begins with this reaffirmation: "The modes of God's presence determine the forms of our encounter with him. If humanity, each man, is the living temple of God, we meet God in our encounter with men" (p. 194).

From this shaky premise a very important conclusion is drawn, but the conclusion is as shaky as the premise. "The conclusion follows the weaker premise," says classical logic, and the principle still applies to the correctness of man's thinking. When Gutiérrez says "each man is the living temple of God," and does not qualify his statement, is he including the oppressors and the unjust? If a human being consciously and deliberately maintains a sinful situation or cultivates institutionalized violence, can he too be said to be "the living temple of God"? When Gutiérrez pronounces that "history is the living temple of God" and that "the profane no longer exists," has he thought of the history of oppression in which so many millions of men have been dehumanized? Or of a situation in which God is explicitly excluded, insulted, dishonored, and eliminated, while man is mistreated, humiliated, tortured, and trodden down? How can anyone say the profane no longer exists? Is there nothing profane about Dachau, Auschwitz, and the countless other concentration camps now scattered about the world?

St. Paul was the first to say that the baptized person is a living temple of God, but it would never have occurred to him to claim that "humanity, every man, history, is the living temple of God." Very much the contrary, for he makes his statement only of the baptized who are "holy and immaculate" and do not profane the temple. For Paul's real meaning, we need only read 1 Corinthians 3:16–17 or 6:14–20, or even Ephesians 2:20–22.

> Can you not realize that the unholy will not fall heir to the kingdom of God? Do not deceive yourselves: no fornicators, idolators, or adulterers, no sodomites, thieves, misers, or drunkards, no slanderers or robbers will inherit God's kingdom. And such were some of you; but you have been washed, consecrated, justified in the name of our Lord Jesus Christ and in the Spirit of our God [1 Cor 6:9–11, cf. Gal 5:21].

If "humanity, every man, history, is the living temple of God," it is impossible to make sense of this other apostolic exhortation:

> Do not yoke yourselves in a mismatch with unbelievers. After all, what do righteousness and lawlessness have in common, or what fellowship can light have with darkness? What accord is there between Christ and Belial, what common lot between believer and unbeliever? Tell me what agreement there is between the temple of God and idols [2 Cor 6:14–16].

Gustavo Gutiérrez is certainly correct when he tells us that "the doctrine of pure nature has been completely abandoned in contemporary theology" (p. 75, no. 21); but he could have added that "pure nature" was never accepted in Catholic theology as having been realized as a historical fact. He is also correct when he says that "historically and concretely we know man only as actually called to meet God" (p. 71). All sound Catholic theologians teach this, and have always taught it. But none of this provides a premise for a thesis that "history is one." The fact that God calls all men does not mean that all men have responded, are now responding, or will respond to this call or universal vocation, so as to build, with God, a single history that would be the history of salvation.

Gutiérrez speaks of a "rediscovery of this single convocation to salvation" (p. 71), but there has been no "rediscovery": the universal call to salvation has been the common teaching of theologians ever since St. Paul proclaimed the universal salvific will of God. Less common, however, is this other statement: "All men are in Christ efficaciously called to communion with God" (p. 71). "Efficaciously" (the word makes us think of "efficacious grace") is not so evident. In any case, since, according to Gutiérrez, "the single vocation to salvation" is true "beyond all distinctions" (p. 72) and since "vocation" is already an *efficacious* call, he can easily draw this important conclusion: "To participate in the process of liberation is already, in a certain sense, a salvific work" (p. 72).

The defenders of a monistic history are certainly right in saying that according to the plan of God, or in the economy God wants, there *should* be but a single history. In saying this, however, they give the impression that they completely overlook the action within this history either of sinful man, who sets himself against the fulfillment of the divine plan, or of the "mystery of iniquity" which acts alongside, and against, the "mystery of salvation" and thus creates a kind of parallel history. It is not dualism to say that God and the devil exist. We have been very much aware of this ever since St. Augustine's debates with the Manicheans. "All of human life, whether individual or collective, shows itself to be a dramatic struggle between good and evil, between light and darkness" (*GS*, 13c/211).

For a monumental struggle against the powers of darkness pervades the whole history of man. The battle was joined from the very origins of the world and will continue until the last day, as the Lord has attested. Caught in this conflict, man is obliged to wrestle constantly if he is to cling to what is good. Nor can he achieve his own integrity without valiant efforts and the help of God's grace [*GS*, 37b/235].

The history of sinful man is not identical with the history of the unfolding divine plan. Not everything historical is salvific; not everything human is Christian. "Not every concept of liberation is necessarily consistent with the Gospel vision of man, things, and events."[80]

The truth taught by the Christian faith is that throughout human history *two forces* are engaged in "a monumental struggle" until the *parousia*. Each force has "its" history.

12. The Human Sciences in Theology

In the literature of Christians for Socialism the discussion of many religious topics, especially under the heading of the proclaimed but difficult task of reformulating the faith (assuming that "reformulation" does not mean simple denial), is reduced to mere questions of method. There is talk, when this happens, of using the human sciences (in place of philosophy) as the necessary and sufficient tool of theological reflection. We are told that, in the past, the formulations of the faith were conditioned by historical situations, cultural preferences, social demands, juridical structures, unscientific concepts of nature, empirical knowledge of man, and so forth. There is a good deal of truth in all this.

There undoubtedly were nontheological and purely pragmatic factors that influenced, sometimes in a decisive manner, the form of a tradition, the shape of an institution, or the formulation of a doctrine. Nonetheless, these traditions, institutions, and doctrines are in many cases also and indeed primarily theological and, as such, cannot and should not be analyzed solely in terms of the human sciences. Even as we admit the evidence of historical development, we must always ask whether the development corresponds to an inner exigency of the Gospel rather than simply to historical and human factors of a nontheological kind. The Gospel, for its part, is not reducible to a datum of history or society; it is the word of Jesus Christ, and is believed and lived by a Church that the Holy Spirit guides and helps.

The New Testament may not give us sufficiently explicit and precise information on the origins of an institution (papacy, episcopate, presbyterate, diaconate) or a tradition (liturgical traditions, e.g.) or a doctrine (original sin, living fellowship with our departed brothers and sisters, etc.). However, this fact alone does not solve the problem of the validity or truth of these traditions, institutions, and doctrines. The fact is not even necessarily a premise that allows us to say that, with regard to these institutions, doctrines, and traditions, we are free to think as we please, or that all these traditions and so forth are a purely human or purely ecclesiastical creation.

For example, it does not seem possible to prove from the text of the New Testament that only the apostles and their ordained successors can preside at the Eucharist; but neither can it be proved from the New Testament that any and every baptized Christian can preside at the Eucharist. Perhaps we cannot prove that the Twelve exercised their authority without the consent of the community, but neither can we prove that they had to have the prior consent of the community. Perhaps we cannot prove that the Twelve determined that their *exousia* ("power," i.e., their capacity to exercise the ministry) should be passed on only to bishops as their successors, but neither can we prove that they regarded all the baptized as bearers of the apostolic *exousia*.

Examples could be multiplied, and the reason for this state of affairs is quite simple. The New Testament writings originated in the preaching of the Gospel and were at the service of this preaching. They are not set over and against tradition (the apostolic *paradosis*) but are part of it, without becoming completely coextensive with "the tradition that comes from the apostles" (*DV*, 8b/116). This is why Vatican II insists once again on the principle that "it is not from sacred Scripture alone that the Church draws her certainty about everything which has been revealed" (*DV*, 9/117). The apostolic Church did not originate in a detailed exegetical or critico-historical analysis of the New Testament writings. Neither does the Church depend for her nature and constitution on the critico-historical method or on any other human science, much less on the Marxist tools of analysis. It is simply absurd to imply that Christians must hope in Karl Marx (who, besides, was not a Latin American).

For the Christian, who believes in a God unlike the god of the deists — a God who is indeed transcendent but is also immanent — the history of the world and mankind, and especially the history of salvation and the Church, is not a closed system. The factors which explain its development, the reasons for its existence, and the finality that governs it are not purely immanent; that is, they are not found exclusively within this history itself. The acknowledgment that nontheological or purely pragmatic factors (often sociological, psychological, and historical) sometimes play a decisive role should not make us forget the existence of other factors which are equally decisive but purely theological and, as such, elude the perception and analysis of the historian, the sociologist, the Marxist, the psychologist, and even the exegete, and are perceived solely by faith and in the light of faith.

God calls man to be the master and king of creation, but man is not therefore his own end or the sole or principal artificer and creator of his own history, much less that of the Church. His history is also shaped by the unforeseeable action of the transcendent God, the Lord of history, and by the fact that this history is oriented toward the "eschaton." We Christians must never forget what the Apostle reveals to us concerning the presence and action of the "mystery of iniquity": "the secret force of lawlessness is already at work" (2 Thes 2:7, cf. vv. 3–8). It is only with this "eschatological proviso" constantly in mind that the Christian can involve himself in history, sociology, or psychology.

The Gospel may never be cut off from history and the sociological and psychological conditions which history makes inevitable. This does not mean, however, that the Gospel is simply a datum for the historian, the sociologist, and the psychologist, or that it can be exhaustively judged by the human sciences, no matter how scrupulously they may approach the subject. Consequently, in studying the Gospel and its essential requirements we should indeed call upon the help of the historians, the sociologists, the exegetes, and the students of the other human sciences. Yet it is not for these scientists and scholars, as such, to say the final, much less the decisive word. That word belongs to those who live the Gospel and believe in the word of God; it belongs to the humble and the lowly, to whom alone the Father reveals the mysteries of his kingdom (cf. Mt 11:25–26). From the others, the "learned and clever" — unless they be also humble men of faith — these realities are hidden by the Father; it is not given to them to know the mysteries of the kingdom of heaven (cf. Mt 13:11).

13. There Is No "Latin American" Ontology

The work of "liberating" the consciences of the Christian masses (a task the promoters of the "Church of the People" claim for themselves) is an astonishingly superficial business. It is contrary, moreover, to the whole of the tradition received from the apostles, and it utterly mistakes the nature of man and the laws that govern his nature. In the view of these people, of course, even to speak of natural laws is to "ideologize," but this is because they are intellectually schizophrenic (they cannot understand the distinction between duality and dualism and, therefore, see and denounce dichotomies everywhere) and theologically paranoid (they feel themselves constantly pursued by the phantom of ideologization). The Marxist bug has poisoned them and made them sick.

The nature of man (and other living things) is compatible with development (which may take the form of decadence) and change. But as long as man remains man, he does not change radically, completely, and in every respect. Something of him remains constant through all the change, and it is precisely because of this "something" that man continues to be man. He continues to be man, whether in Europe or in Latin America, whether in this culture or in that, whether in the present century or in some past or future age. There is, then, a certain minimum of ontology that is universally valid, a certain minimal ontological structure without which man would not be what he is or would cease to be what he is. With the aid of and within that structure, he can and must act and develop himself so as to realize all his potentialities as the being he is, without changing into some other kind of being. Development is possible only on the basis of something permanent. That is why Vatican II asserts unhesitatingly: "The Church also maintains that beneath all changes there are many realities which do not change" (*GS,* 10h/208).

To deny that amid historical change and contingency there exists something abiding, necessary, and universally valid is to fall into solipsism or utter subjectivism. The denial would also entail a radical denial of the faith, since everything about Scripture and the Councils is "historical" and, therefore, historically conditioned. Such concepts as "personal God, creator and judge," "man, creature of God," "covenant," "sin," "salvation," or "Jesus, Messiah and Son of God," are historical concepts that were conditioned by the Hebrew culture in which they developed. Are we to conclude from this that since we no longer live in that culture and environment, the concepts no longer have meaning and value for us? Or that we know of nothing that is valid for all times, cultures, and human beings? To say so would be to deny the faith, but also to assert the impossibility of communication.

Let us take a specific example. In the Letter to the Romans the Apostle speaks of certain sexual activities as "unnatural" and others as "natural," and he denounces the former as shameful and as leading to man's exclusion from the kingdom of God (1:26–27, cf. 1 Cor 6:9). Paul's manner of speaking is very much conditioned by his Hebrew culture (since he presupposes the concepts of a personal God who creates and judges, of sin, and the kingdom of God) or by Greek culture (he presupposes the concepts of nature and what is in accord with or contrary to nature). Evidently, we cannot simply call attention to or emphasize this historical fact and then immediately conclude that the norm used by the Apostle is not valid for other times and cultures, or that we Latin Americans are dispensed from it because we have emancipated ourselves from European culture. Before we can draw such a conclusion, we must show that the norm in question, in the mind of Paul, was intrinsically and substantially dependent on concepts which were current at the time but were also purely contingent upon that culture or cultures (as was, e.g., the prohibition against eating the meat of strangled animals, in Acts 15:29).

Thus it is that, thousands of years later and in circumstances that are utterly different *but still human,* the believer finds teaching, guidance, and counsel in words that were spoken concerning problems that were not precisely the same as his *but were nonetheless human.* Man's problems are, at bottom, still the same because of that "abiding something" in virtue of which man remains man.

14. But There Are Latin American Problems

It is often asserted that in Latin America we have two parallel theologies: one "European," the other "Latin American." Those who exalt "Latin American" theology heap scorn on "European" theology.

It must be granted that, as a matter of fact, those who teach the various theological disciplines in Latin America received their training elsewhere, usually in Europe. Consequently, even when they are Latin Americans, they teach a European theology and frequently come in conflict with what is now called "Latin American theology." The authors of this "Latin American theology" are either not trained as theologians or, if they are Europeans or Latin Americans trained in Europe, they try to forget the theology they learned and to adopt the "Latin American theology."

It must also be granted that, as a matter of fact, Latin America is experiencing situations and problems which are unknown in Europe and which require light from theology or can be the starting point for a new theological reflection. Within the unity of a universally valid and catholic theology there is, and must be, diversity. Of theology we can say what Vatican II says of the Church: that it is both universal or catholic and particular or local. "In virtue of this catholicity each individual part of the Church contributes through its special gifts to the good of the other parts and of the whole Church. Thus through the common sharing of gifts and through the common effort to attain fullness in unity, the whole and each of the parts receive increase" (*LG,* 13c/31).

The same holds for theology:

> If this goal is to be achieved, theological investigation must necessarily be stirred up in each major socio-cultural area, as it is called. In this way, under the light of the tradition of the universal Church, a fresh scrutiny will be brought to bear on the deeds and words which God has made known, which have been consigned to sacred Scripture, and which have been unfolded by the Church Fathers and the teaching authority of the Church.
>
> Thus it will be more clearly seen in what ways faith can seek for understanding in the philosophy and wisdom of these peoples. A better view will be gained of how their customs, outlook on life, and social order can be reconciled with the manner of living taught by divine revelation. As a result, avenues will be opened for a

more profound adaptation in the whole area of Christian life [*AG*, 22b–c/612].

In the light of these statements, the ideal would be to establish in Latin America a very good faculty of theology that would train our professors of theology. That will not be easy. As a temporary solution, therefore, we should think of a kind of "graduate school of theology" which all should attend who have received their training at a faculty outside Latin America and who wish to, or are destined to, teach theology in Latin America.

15. The Poor

The poor are the reason why all the movements for a "Church of the People" have come into existence. What could be more worthy and fitting for a true Christian than to live for the poor and helpless, the sick and abandoned, the suffering and the sorrowing! This has been the concern of the Church since apostolic times. Only those who are ignorant of Church history can deny it — or those who refuse to see the countless proofs of it, past and present: thousands upon thousands of saints, canonized or uncanonized; countless self-sacrificing missionaries who, with extraordinary generosity, have left native land, family, possessions, and comfort to live as poor amid the poor and suffering; millions of religious women — what an extraordinary army they form! — who toil and exhaust themselves in total dedication to the sick, the orphan, the elderly, and so many others who are abandoned, outcast, and poor.

Any good history of the Church will document these activities which have characterized the Church's life in every age, and which have characterized her life in Latin America ever since the continent was discovered. It would be unforgivable nearsightedness to see in the Church and her bishops, priests, religious, and actively apostolic laity nothing more than a "bourgeoisie" who connive with the powerful and the exploiters. That kind of person has indeed existed, but he has not been the rule. For "the Church, embracing sinners in her bosom, is at the same time holy and always in need of being purified, and incessantly pursues the path of penance and renewal" (*LG*, 8d/24).

It is certainly not *because* they are so concerned about the poor that serious objections are raised against those who, in a somewhat triumphalistic tone, announce that they have made "an option for the poor." What is disturbing and worrisome about them is not their concern for the suffering, but the ideology they profess with regard to the "oppressed" and the action, based on that ideology, which they undertake in order to "transform" society. As we have seen, everything about their approach is simplistic: they simplistically divide mankind into only two groups or classes, the poor and the rich. With the same simplism, they assert that the poor are the oppressed and the rich the oppressors, and they seem to think that every poor person, by the fact of being poor, is oppressed, while every rich person, by the fact of being rich, is an oppressor. In just as simplistic a way, they imagine that once the poor have attained to power (the real goal of the "Church of the People"), they will not be rich or oppressors of others. Since, in their view, Jesus Christ himself was poor and made an option for the poor (they call him "the subversive of Nazareth" [24/no. 20]), and even declared that the kingdom of heaven belongs to the poor, they possess some ready-made and seemingly Christian premises for their ideology.

We shall not enter into complicated questions that properly belong to sociology and economics, and are certainly not to be solved by facile and uncritical identifications of the poor with the oppressed, the poor and oppressed with the people, and the rich with the oppressor. We shall simply offer some brief remarks on the exegetico-theological problem of the "poor" in the Bible and especially in the Gospel. These remarks will help us grasp the

Christian and evangelical meaning of a good, sound, balanced "Church of the People" such as we all desire.

It will be profitable to recall, as a first point, that poverty and oppression constitute a social state which is utterly contrary to the Lord's will and is therefore not a necessary condition for hearing and understanding his word. On the contrary, the non-poor person (let us avoid the loaded term "rich man"), the person who achieves human fulfillment and happiness and who is healthy and joyful, is precisely the one whose life is most in conformity with the divine plan for man. Christ does not want us to be wretched, much less oppressed: "For your sake he made himself poor though he was rich, so that you might become rich by his poverty" (2 Cor 8:9).

The Hebrew words *anaw* ("poor"; Latin Vulgate, *pauper;* Greek, *ptöchos*), *anawim* ("poor" in the plural; Vulgate, *pauperes*), and *anawah* ("poverty"; Vulgate, *paupertas;* Greek, *ptöcheia*) have a primarily moral and religious meaning. The *anawim* of the Psalms, the wisdom literature, and the prophets are the humble people who reverence the Lord, have recourse to him, seek him, and place their trust in him. For this reason they are rightly regarded as the true "Israel," the people of God and the heirs of the promises. They are the holy and upright people who so often meet with misfortune and humiliation but do not, on that account, cease to serve God. Their spiritual outlook is summed up in the words of Psalm 37:7: "Be quiet before Yahweh, and wait patiently for him" (the Jerusalem Bible).

The contrary attitude is that of the proud, the self-assured, the wicked, those who trust in themselves, who are arrogant, conceited, insolent, and lacking in Christian humility. In a study of the Beatitudes, Jacques Dupont calls attention to the fact that the fathers of the Church interpreted "the poor in spirit" as meaning the humble and modest, but that they did not explain how the idea of poverty turned into the idea of humility.[81] He says that modern exegetes had been perplexed at not finding the expression "the poor in spirit" in other literature of the time. The situation has now changed, however, since the texts from Qumran, which date from the time of Jesus, use the expression "poor in spirit" (*anawim ruah*) in contexts which leave no doubt about its real meaning. The fathers of the Church were correct: the "poor in spirit" are the humble; the attitude of soul in the phrase "in spirit" is interior humility; and it is biblically correct to speak of "spiritual poverty." This is a fact about the Bible, not a later bit of bourgeois ideologization.

In another study of the Beatitudes (or "macarisms," as they are also called, from the Greek word for "blessed," *makarios*), Maximiliano García Cordero compared the versions of Matthew and Luke.[82] He points out that, in the view of the Bible, the man who is poor or indigent gains no advantage over the rich man, as far as entry into the kingdom of God is concerned, if his ambition is to become rich and live a life of pleasure like the rich liver or the rich fool of the parables (Lk 12:16–20, 16:19–21). Matthew seems to be inspired, in his "poor in spirit," by the ideal of the "poor man of Yahweh" of whom Psalm 34 speaks: "A cry goes up from the poor man, and Yahweh hears him" (v. 6, JB). This poor man is described as one who fears Yahweh (v. 7), takes shelter in him (v. 8), seeks him (v. 10), is contrite of heart (v. 18), and serves him and looks to him for refuge (v. 22). Matthew certainly has in mind a spirit of detachment that is based on this ideal of the "poor of Yahweh," since the latter were better prepared than others to enter into a kingdom that demands sacrifices and renunciation (cf. Acts 14:22: "We must undergo many trials if we are to enter into the reign of God"). The difficulties the rich face in this respect are well brought out in the parable of the sower: "What was sown among briers is the man who hears the message, but then worldly anxiety and the lure of money choke it off. Such a one produces no yield."

In Matthew 5:3, Christ uses the word "poor" with moral overtones that had already been heard in Zephaniah 2:3: "Seek the Lord, all you humble of the earth, who have observed his law; seek justice, seek humility."

We may also note that Matthew tones down the more radical (and therefore more archaic) formulation of Luke, so as not to stir up social resentment in a religious community that contained both rich and poor (Jas 1:10–11, 2:5–13, 4:13). This kind of "spiritualization" (which is the doing, be it noted, of the Gospel itself and not of a later "bourgeoisified" Church) is more in keeping with the general thrust of the Gospel, which rejects all forms of rancor and class struggle.

What the Beatitudes really urge upon us, then, is the spiritual disposition of openness to the kingdom of God, for, as Mary says in her Magnificat, "He [God] has . . . raised the lowly to high places" (Lk 1:53). The lowly or humble know that they are and always will be beggars before God, and it is from him that they hope for everything. The kingdom of God is barred to anyone who is willing to be a slave of money and attached to it as to life's supreme good. The rich man is always in great danger of embracing the life of luxury and turning away from the basic demands of the Gospel message. The person who has developed the spiritual attitude of renunciation evidently lives in true poverty and without attachment to real or possible riches. This kind of "poor" man finds himself, in principle, in a much better situation when it comes to accepting the renunciations required by the reign of God, as did the apostles, who left all they had, unlike the rich young man who did not have the courage to leave his great wealth behind him and follow Jesus when invited to do so (Mt 19:22–23).

It is undeniable that Christ "spiritualized" (in the "Church of the People" they would say "ideologized") the false hopes of an earthly messianism that aimed at immediate socio-economic progress. He made it clear that he had come to fill spiritual, not material, needs. He had come not to change unjust social structures but to heal the human heart of its propensity for greed, pleasure, and violence. As Jesus saw it, love, not hatred and class struggle, must reform society. For him, the reform of society begins not in social structures but in the heart of man: "Wicked designs come from the deep recesses of the heart: acts of fornication, theft, murder, adulterous conduct, greed, maliciousness, deceit, sensuality, envy, blasphemy, arrogance an obtuse spirit. All these evils come from within and render a man impure" (Mk 7:21–23).

The exegetes also point out that while Jesus speaks often of the danger of wealth (cf. Mt 6:19–20, 16:25–26, Lk 16:13, Mk 8: 35–36), he never condemns it without qualification. He does indeed condemn the greedy rich man who exploits the poor. This same Jesus, however, had friends in high Jewish society, men like Nicodemus and Joseph of Arimathea (Jn 3:1–21, 19:38), and he did not require that they dispossess themselves of their possessions in order to be his disciples.

For these various reasons, our word "poor" is not a faithful translation of the Hebrew *anaw,* nor can it convey the rich meaning of the biblical concept. The Blessed Virgin Mary, who probably was not one of the poor and exploited, was nonetheless an *anaw,* a "servant of the Lord" (Lk 1:38). Vatican II says of her that "she stands out among the poor and humble of the Lord, who confidently await and receive salvation from Him" (*LG,* 55b/87), which certainly does not mean liberation from material poverty or social oppression. Moreover, in giving his salvation God looks to the *anawah* or "lowliness" (humility) of his servant (Lk 1:48).

In Matthew 11:25 Jesus praises the Father because "what you have hidden from the learned and the clever you have revealed to the merest children." The "merest children" who receive and understand the revelation of the mysteries of the kingdom (cf. Mt 13:11) are precisely the lowly or humble: those who, like Christ, are "gentle and humble of heart" (Mt 11:29). Material poverty, oppression, or captivity of any kind are not the decisive factors. Nathanael does not seem to have been poor, and yet the Lord says of him: "This man is a true Israelite. There is no guile in him" (Jn 1:47). He was not poor, but he was *anaw,* as were Lazarus and his sisters Martha and Mary, who, though not poor, were friends of Jesus. The same can be said of the women who, according to Luke 8:3, assisted Jesus "out of their means."

If, then, we want to divide mankind into two classes as seen by Jesus or the Gospel, we would have, on one side, the "merest children," that is, the humble *anawim.* (People who are materially poor clearly have a greater subjective inclination to belong to this class, but they are not the only ones, since there are also humble rich people.) On the other side we would have the proud. (People who are materially wealthy, men of authority and power, and the well educated have a greater subjective inclination to belong to this class, but they are not the only ones, since there are also proud poor people.)

God's interventions in the history of salvation seem to follow a pattern: "God is stern with the arrogant but to the humble he shows kindness" (1 Pt 5:5), or "Everyone who exalts himself shall be humbled and he who humbles himself shall be exalted" (Lk 14:11). This accounts for the advice Jesus gives his disciples: "Let the greater among you be as the junior, the leader as the servant" (Lk 22:26). On this point, the divine Teacher is unsparing: "I assure you, unless you change and become like little children, you will not enter the kingdom of God" (Mt 18:3).

It is the humble, then — not those who are simply materially poor — who are the true members of the authentically Christian Church of the people.

During the Second Vatican Council, Pope John XXIII and a good number of the Council fathers, especially Cardinal Lercaro and Bishop Helder Cámara, spoke with enthusiasm of the "Church of the poor," and even wanted a conciliar text on the subject. The Theological Commission, which was in charge of composing the constitution on the Church, then set up a special subcommission to study a possible text. The result was the present third paragraph of article 8 of the "Constitution on the Church" (paragraph 3 of the Latin text; in English, paragraphs 3 and 4). Because of its ambiguity, the expression "Church of the poor" was not used, and indeed appears nowhere in the conciliar documents.

The text, however, contains the official thinking of the Council on the subject, and three comparisons are made between the mission and action of Christ, and the task of the Church:

1. "Just as Christ carried out the work of redemption in poverty and under oppression, so the Church is called to follow the same path in communicating to men the fruits of salvation" (*LG,* 8c/23).

2. "Christ Jesus, 'though he was by nature God . . . emptied himself, taking the nature of a slave' (Phil 2:6), and 'being rich, he became poor' (2 Cor 8:9) for our sakes. Thus, although the Church needs human resources to carry out her mission, she is not set up to seek earthly glory, but to proclaim humility and self-sacrifice, even by her own example" (ibid.).

3. "Christ was sent by the Father 'to bring good news to the poor, to heal the contrite of heart' (Lk 4:18), 'to seek and to save what is lost' (Lk 19:10). Similarly, the Church encompasses with love all those who are afflicted with human weakness. Indeed, she recognizes in the poor and suffering the likeness of her poor and suffering Founder. She does all she can to relieve their need and in them she strives to serve Christ" (*LG,* 8d/24).

We have undoubtedly a serious obligation to be very sensitive to the cry of the materially oppressed, and yet the Christian, as such, should be even more alert to the despairing cry of poor sinners who are traveling the clear road to eternal damnation (cf. Mt 7:13). The question Jesus asked long ago is directed also to us: "Which is less trouble to say, 'Your sins are forgiven' or 'Stand up and walk'?" (Mt 9:4). It is clear that the mission of Christ as savior, redeemer, and liberator (and therefore also the mission of his body the Church) is first and foremost in this more difficult and exclusively divine area of forgiving sins and reestablishing the lost harmony and friendship between God and sinful man. Rich or poor, captive or free, dependent or independent, capitalist or socialist, healthy or sick, young or old, sad or joyful: these distinctions matter little, since, as far as God is concerned, "all men have sinned and are deprived of the glory of God" (Rom 3:23).

In the "sin of the world" we are all equally sinners, and only the Lamb of God can take sin away (cf. Jn 1:29). "By himself and by his own power, no one is freed from sin or raised above himself, or completely rid of his sickness or his solitude or his servitude. On the contrary, all stand in need of Christ, their Model, their Mentor, their Liberator, their Savior, their Source of life" (*AG,* 8b/595). As Christians who are charged with continuing the work of Christ, our first choice must be to help sinners.

One of the great and consoling truths of revelation is that Christ "died for all" (2 Cor 5:15). However, as the Council of Trent explained in an exercise of its supreme authority, "all do not benefit by his death, but only those to whom the merits of his suffering are communicated."[83] St. Augustine had made the same point long before: "The blood of Christ was shed for you if you want it; if you do not want it, it was not shed for you. . . . The blood of Christ is salvation for him who wants it, and a torment for him who does not."[84]

To communicate the merits of the passion and resurrection of Christ to the greatest number of men in order to unite them to the paschal mystery: such has always been the great task, mission, and duty of the Church. If the Church is to be the visible instrument of the Lord and Savior, or "the universal sacrament of salvation" (*LG,* 48b/79), she must be the Church of all men (in this sense, she is eminently "of the people"), and her radical option is always an option for sinners, whatever be their social and economic situation. Yet her preference, like that of Christ, is for the humble, the lowly, the little people, those who have become "like little children." And within this group, her greatest preference (though it is never exclusive, and still less a "class option") is for the poor, the abandoned, the sick, the orphaned, the elderly.

In a "Circular Letter" published by "Chilean priests who love their country and their priesthood," we read this very theological formulation of a commitment:

Our commitment to Chile can be summed up in a few words: to

be priests. Priests without adjectives or epithets. Our priesthood is not limited to a single territory, nor is it at the service of a single ideology, faction, party, or class to the exclusion of others. We are priests of the Christ who came and died for people of all races, nations, and conditions.[85]

16. Unanswered Questions about the Praxis of Liberation

The following list of unanswered questions is the result of critical reflection on various theological or ideological attitudes, tendencies, and essays of Christians who are struggling, or want to struggle, for the economic and social liberation of the Latin American poor. Their positions and assertions involve a number of problems that have thus far received no adequate solution and require further study and clarification. The questions can be distributed under three headings.

Questions about the Point of Departure

The process of analyzing the situation in Latin America includes:

a) The establishment of the fact that there exists a situation of poverty and even penury, and of its extent. On this point there are no special problems requiring theological reflection.

b) A diagnosis of this situation. Here we find three positions: (1) The cause of the poverty is underdevelopment; the solution is action that will help toward development; (2) The cause is the social marginalization of the poor; the solution is to integrate them into society; (3) The cause is the dependence of the poor and the domination of the powerful, rich, and oppressive over the poor, wretched, and oppressed; the solution is action or struggle for liberation.

Many of our Christians (lay people and ordained ministers) accept the third position, which starts from a supposed general situation of dependence). They maintain that help for development has proved useless (and they reject this course as paternalistic "developmentalism"), and that integration is not a viable solution (it suggests that the present social system is healthy in itself or at least that it can be corrected). In analyzing the situation these Christians use the Marxist analytic method which (they claim) is scientific and therefore, because truth is one, is and must be compatible with the Christian message.

There is no denying that many of the Latin American poor live in a situation of dependence on and exploitation by their fellow men (a "sinful situation" and, as such, a necessary subject for Christian prophetism or denunciation) and that they must therefore be liberated. But, even when this is admitted, a number of questions remain.

1. Is dependence in fact the sole cause of our poverty and wretchedness?

2. Is this dependence in fact basically economic?

3. Are not underdevelopment and marginalization also a direct cause and often the only cause of many situations of wretched poverty? To what extent and in what areas are these factors actually dominant?

4. Therefore, is not action for the development or for the integration of men into society the most adequate solution in areas that are really underdeveloped or marginalized (and not primarily dependent or dominated and exploited)?

5. Is the existing social system in fact intrinsically evil and beyond correction?

6. Is the Marxist analytic method reallv scientific?

7. Can this method be isolated from the other philosophical categories of Marxism?

8. Does not such an analysis of reality take us into pure economicism?

9. Is not the theory of dependence directed too much at foreign dominators (concretely, United States capitalism) as sole or at least principal cause of dependence in Latin America?

Questions about the Means

Many Christians are persuaded that the Latin American situation is one of dependence and not of underdevelopment and lack of integration. They are persuaded, too, that this dependence is basically economic and caused by the capitalist system (the status quo). They maintain, therefore, the necessity of an action or struggle for liberation from the capitalist status quo (which, being a situation of institutionalized injustice and violence is simply a sinful situation), so that a socialist system may be introduced. This change is the "revolution"; it need not be bloody, but an eventual recourse to violence is not excluded. These Christians adopt the theory that society is divided into antagonistic and irreconcilably opposed classes (oppressors and oppressed), with the poor always being the oppressed. Therefore, they openly accept the Marxist concept of a "class struggle," that is, of irreconcilable opposition. Liberation must necessarily come by way of a class struggle ("revolutionary praxis"), and the "Christian commitment" will take the form precisely of active participation in the struggle ("orthopraxis").

A theology based on this definition of liberation takes as the point of departure for all theologizing not an analysis or interpretation of reality but a transformation of reality; this transformation is the authentic "praxis." The praxis of liberation will be not only the point of departure for theology but also the tribunal that judges the truth or falsity of the dogmas and moral principles which have appeared in the history of the Church. The Church did not possess the tools of Marxist analysis and was therefore incapable of correctly understanding the deeper requirements of the Gospel. It fell victim to bourgeois ideology and preached a Christianity that was distorted and manipulated by the ruling, dominant, oppressive classes. The praxis of liberation, then, will provide the horizon within which everything is to be viewed, and will also be the organizing principle for the whole of theology. The subject or agent of theological creation is the same as the subject of the praxis of liberation, namely, the people alone or, more accurately, the people who are aware of being oppressed and who struggle for their liberation.

Here new questions arise.

10. Is there not a possible "third solution" between the capitalist status quo (which exploits man) and socialism (which in fact also exploits man wherever it takes power)?

11. Is the social teaching of the Church in fact purely "reformist"?

12. Are the values by which socialism defines itself also the values manifested by the socialist systems that have actually been established?

13. Are "social conflict" and "class struggle" really synonymous? (The Marxist "class" is defined by the possession, or lack of possession, of the means of production; "social conflicts," which will always exist, have other causes.)

14. Is not the division of human society into only two antagonistic classes (oppressors and oppressed) an oversimplification?

15. Does the Gospel propose a class struggle among Christians or, on the contrary, a "transforming love lived out amid antagonism and alienation"?

16. Can the "poor" of the Gospel really be identified with the

Marxist "proletariat"? Are the messianic promises therefore meant for the proletariat?

17. Is the "poor" person of Latin America always a "proletarian" in the Marxist sense or someone who is "oppressed" in the classist sense?

18. Is violence in revolutionary praxis an attitude compatible with the Gospel?

19. Is it legitimate to identify Christian commitment exclusively with participation in revolutionary praxis in the name of fidelity to the Gospel, so that those not committed to that praxis would be unfaithful to the Christian message?

20. Does the Christian faith not contain values that transcend the political order?

21. Can sin in the proper sense of the word be reduced to economic alienation or social injustice alone?

22. Is liberation from sin possible only by way of political liberation?

23. Does Christian "conversion" necessarily involve taking a revolutionary position in favor of one class and against another?

24. Is it true that authentic Christian faith must express itself always and solely in revolutionary praxis, so that the latter is the only orthopraxis?

25. Is praxis or orthopraxis to be taken only as a criterion for the veracity or credibility of the Gospel message? Or is it to be taken also as the criterion of truth itself (which supposes a purely pragmatic view of truth) and a tribunal from which there is no appeal?

26. Is revolutionary praxis a "theological locus or source"? In what sense? Is it the only source of interpretation and a starting point for a new theology?

27. Is it legitimate to reject universal principles and start exclusively from a commitment to liberation?

28. Does critical reflection on faith as a political praxis of liberation respect the true nature of theological science?

29. Is it true that the only one who theologizes is the poor person or the people insofar as they are committed to the struggle for liberation?

Questions about the Goal

The outcome of the action or struggle for liberation will be a situation in which a "new man" comes into existence. This situation will be one of social equality, brotherhood, corresponsibility, active participation in political and cultural life, and so on. The people thus liberated will be the only true and authentic subject of the "new Church," the "Church of the People," a Church made up of and existing for the people. This Church alone will be capable of liberating consciences, of deideologizing the official institutional Church that embraces all classes, of reappropriating the Scriptures by effecting a more authentic, materialist rereading of the Gospel and thus discovering its original meaning, and of reinterpreting the faith with the help of the social sciences. It will be a class Church, possessing new ways of living the faith and celebrating the Eucharist; it will elaborate a whole new system of sacraments and seek out a new spirituality and new forms of prayer. There is no hope that these various new forms will arise out of the official Church; the revolutionary process is what will make a revolution possible within the Church. The Church must settle for being continually challenged, for it seems in fact to be an obstacle preventing many Christians from realizing their commitment to liberation.

Nonetheless, here again questions arise.

30. Even as we acknowledge the basic equality of men, we

see clearly that they differ in personality, intelligence, inventiveness and initiative, character, will power, physical strength, moral qualities, intellectual preparation, etc. Therefore, is "social equality" (without any social classes), really possible?

31. Even as we proclaim and acknowledge universal and inalienable rights, we see that man's freedom is always a situated freedom, situated by the countless circumstances of life that antedate our individual existence and were not freely chosen by the individual. We see, too, that because of the present extraordinary multiplication of reciprocal relations among men, human groups small and large (the latter include even the richest and most powerful nations, as the oil crisis is making clear) are becoming daily more interdependent. Is, then, the economic and social freedom men dream of (a freedom without any dependence, even economic) really possible?

32. Can the "new man" of the social or socialist utopia be identified with the "new man" proclaimed by Christ and preached by St. Paul?

33. Has sufficient attention been paid to the inevitable ambiguity and ambivalence of the anticipated economic and social well being which the struggle for liberation will supposedly bring about? What of the repeated warnings of Christ and the Apostles concerning the rich of this world and those whose bellies are full?

34. Does temporal progress have anything to do with the central content of the reign of God which Christ proclaimed? To what extent is such progress at the service of God's reign? To what extent may it be directed to that service?

35. Is it not true that, as the Second Vatican Council teaches, "a monumental struggle against the powers of darkness pervades the whole history of man. The battle was joined from the very origins of the world and will continue until the last day, as the

Lord has attested" (*GS,* 37b/235); and that "the secret force of lawlessness is already at work" (2 Thess 2:7)?

36. Is not social and economic utopianism, which identifies man's liberation with his economic and social liberation, directly contrary to the very essence of the Gospel?

37. Are the social sciences really an adequate instrument for a sound theology satisfying the deepest demands of the human mind?

38. Is it true that the word of God would have no meaning in a situation of social liberation (no poor, no oppressed, no society needing transformation), in which there would be no reason for a theology of "liberation" nor any possibility of a Church of the "poor" nor any need of praxis (transformative activity) or orthopraxis?

39. Does not the steady emphasis on the existential aspect of revelation (its meaning "for us") lead to an undervaluing of its ontological dimension (its meaning "in itself")?

40. Does not the concentration on the social and temporal or historical dimension of faith lead to forgetfulness of its personal and eternal dimension?

41. Amid the emphasis on man as artisan and creator of his own history, is sufficient attention paid to the fact that the final goal of that history, namely the eschaton, has already been determined by the Lord of history?

42. Can the encounter with God and Christ be identified exclusively with participation in a very limited kind of revolutionary process?

43. Can membership in the Church depend on one's political option?

44. Is the poor person in fact the only way to encounter Christ?

45. Is it certain that the faith, as given to us and formulated for us by the Church, originated in a bourgeois society?

46. Has the Church throughout its history always been on the side of the oppressors?

47. Is the "new Church" or "Church of the people" still the Catholic Church that has come down to us from the Apostles?

48. Is a concept of Church unity theologically acceptable when it claims that this unity must be mediated through the unity of mankind, that is, a human unity without social classes?

49. Does the correct understanding of the Gospel really depend on the Marxist method?

50. Does a materialist rereading of the Gospel grasp the spiritual core of Christ's message?

51. Can a revolutionary Jesus be the same as Jesus of Nazareth?

52. Can the history of salvation be simply identified with profane history?

53. Does not the much praised orthopraxis lead almost imperceptibly to a heteropraxis?

Conclusion: Theology or Ideology?

Finally, as a general unanswered question, we may ask whether the type of reflection on the praxis of liberation we have been examining, even when done by Christians, is still genuinely Christian and theological or is it, on the contrary, purely ideological and unconcerned about fidelity to the Lord, his message, and his body which is the Church.

In a review of the theology of liberation[86] Segundo Galilea insists on the need of defining and distinguishing the theology of liberation from other forms of reflection on liberation "which are not theological and which are quite numerous" (p. 14). He then suggests this distinction: "There is, in the proper sense, the theology of liberation which, like every theology, is concerned with faith and evangelization. Then there is also the kind of reflection by Christians on liberation which is to be located rather at the ideological, sociopolitical, pedagogical level." This second level, he says, "is not properly theological nor concerned with faith and the Gospel." He adds:

> Confusions stems from the fact that in the minds of many every reflection on liberation, whether or not it is theological, is already a "theology of liberation": proclamations, pamphlets, statements of Christian groups that deal in any way with "liberation." . . . The confusion of the two levels — that of the theologians of liberation and that of Christians who engage in sociopolitical discussions or social denunciations with regard to liberation — has harmed the theology of liberation by drawing down upon it criticisms that really have nothing to do with it, or by seeming to identify it with political statements that lack any satisfactory theological or pastoral dimension.

What Galilea does not sufficiently emphasize, however, is that the people who formulate such an ideology of liberation (not a theology of liberation) loudly claim to be proposing a "theology" of liberation and to be basing their views on such a theology (cf. 8/370; 31/p. 37). Galilea likewise fails to tell us how we are to react to a non-theological discussion which is "located rather at the ideological, sociopolitical, pedagogical level," when it makes assertions or reaches conclusions that are contrary to Christian faith or the teaching of our Church, that is, when such a discussion moves into the area of theology, even without any intention of theologizing.

Galilea later describes three tendencies in the "theology" of liberation, but without citing a single name or representative work in each category; he leaves each reader the freedom to choose the name or work that best fits the category. He then adds a fourth tendency (p. 28) that is not a form of theology, nor does it have any theological standing, but rather is to be considered an "ideology of liberation." He describes it as follows:

> By and large, this tendency presupposes a certain kind of analysis and ideology; it is a Marxist type of thinking. We do not find ourselves here in the area of the theology of liberation; I do not think that this tendency can be regarded in any proper sense as theological. Although it is a minority trend, it has found numerous exponents in Latin America, especially in the form of various documents and as the latent "theology" of some groups. In this type of thinking, ecclesiology is almost nonexistent, and when it does find expression it is very defective.
>
> In my judgment, many critics of the theology of liberation, whether well informed or not, have leveled their heavy guns at this type of thinking (and rightly so), but without sufficiently defining the important ways in which it differs from the first three tendencies. What some critics point to as "the" theology of liberation that is predominant in Latin America is in fact this fourth type of thinking which has no theological standing.

All this is well said; it is quite accurate and to the point. Galilea's judgment is weighty and apodictic. But here again he fails to point out that it is these "ideologues of liberation," and not their critics, who present their views on the praxis of liberation as a "theology" of liberation. The critics (they too remain prudently anonymous) would like to know who is who in the theology or ideology of liberation, and who these ideologues are who claim to be "Christian" and have no theological standing and no ecclesiology, but nonetheless endeavor to identify their ideology with the theology of liberation, thus leading the faithful into confusion, perplexity, and even the denial of many parts of the faith.

This Report has been concerned not with the theologians of liberation but with the ideologues who have no theological standing. It has also endeavored to identify them as groups or individuals.

And Pope Paul VI tells us:

> The Church connects but never equates human liberation with salvation in Jesus Christ. For she knows from divine revelation, historical experience, and reflection on the faith that not every concept of liberation is necessarily consistent with the Gospel vision of man, things, and events. She knows that the acquisition of liberation, prosperity and development is not enough to bring about the reign of God.
>
> The Church is, moreover, thoroughly convinced that any temporal or political liberation contains within itself the seeds of its own negation and must fail to achieve the lofty ideal it sets itself. For its true motive is not the establishment of justice in charity, and its driving passion is not spiritual virtue or the winning of eternal salvation and blessedness in God as a final goal. None of this is changed by the fact that the liberation movement tries to justify itself by one or other passage of the Old and New Testaments; that it thinks its theoretical postulates and norms of action are supported by theological principles and conclusions; or that it believes itself to be the theology for our times.
>
> The Church certainly considers it highly important to establish structures which are more human, more just, more respectful of the rights of the person, less oppressive and less coercive. She knows, however, that even the most perfect structures and the most ideal systems quickly become inhuman unless the inhuman bent of man's heart is corrected, unless those who live in or control these structures are converted in heart and mind.[87]

Appendix: Evangelization and Liberation, According to the Synod of Bishops, 1974

The Synod of Bishops, 1974, at which I was a "special assistant to the secretary," managed to give us a final declaration of only about six pages. But then, everyone knows that the purpose of the Synod as presently constituted (it is a purely consultative body, without deliberative power) is not to issue documents or concluding declarations to the universal Church. The Synods of 1967, 1969, and 1971 did, however, issue such statements, and the Synod of 1974 followed suit; it wanted to issue a declaration on evangelization in the present-day world. The few pages it produced are not, and were not meant to be, the sole result of the Synod.[1]

The fact that the Synod could not produce anything better or more substantial for a final declaration was due to the method adopted for the work of the assembly. The Fathers at the Synod of 1971 had felt the same defect of method, and had spoken out strongly against it, but to no avail. In 1974, the method was even less satisfactory. For this reason the Fathers at this Synod were again unsparing of harsh criticism.

The problem seems to be inherent, however, in the very nature of the Synod. What is a Synod of Bishops for? The *motu proprio* by which Pope Paul VI established the Synod says: "The Synod of Bishops has, of its very nature, the function of providing information and offering advice."[2] To provide information and offer advice to the Pope. The Synod of 1974 certainly provided information, freely and at great length, not only to the Pope but to all who were in the synodal meeting hall. I cannot say whether it also "offered advice"; the "dry list" of sixty-seven questions discussed at this session was given to the Pope, but it cannot be said to have "offered advice" to him.

On the other hand, Pope Paul was almost always present in person as the bishops of the world spoke of their experiences and, as the spokesmen for the twelve language groups, conveyed to the full assembly the results of their conversations and discussions. The Pope was actively present, moreover; by this I mean that he had before him a photocopy of each address and report, and made his own annotations on it. It is these addresses and reports that contain the real riches of the Synod, for in them speaks the experience of the bishops from every continent. In them we find their pastoral preoccupations, their doctrinal and theological concerns, their desires for greater fidelity to the Gospel, to God's will, to the inspirations of the Holy Spirit, to the signs of the times, and to real men in their present situation. This last means: to secularized man in the North Atlantic countries; to the as yet animistic but now decolonized man of Africa; to the man of the great traditional religions of Asia; to man reduced to silence in the socialist countries; and to man yearning for greater social, economic, political, and cultural liberation in Latin America.

These addresses and reports are a rich mine, and cannot be left in the archives of the synodal secretariat. They must be researched and studied. As the Pope said in his closing address: "These [elements of response to various problems] need . . . to be unified and examined more thoroughly."[3] It will be well worth the trouble to study patiently all that the Fathers of the Synod said, on the action of the Holy Spirit in the Church and outside her, on the need of proclaiming the Gospel and accompanying the proclamation with personal witness; on the difficulties which some ecclesiastical institutions are putting in the way of evangelization; on the local or particular Churches (a major theme of the Synod) ; on the pressing need of greater adaptation or "indigenization" of the Gospel message; on the religiosity of the masses; on the relations between evangelization and human progress or liberation; on small ecclesial base communities; on the causes of religious indifferentism in Catholics who do not practice their faith; on the problems of youth; on the evangelizing and ministerial role of women; on the need of greater collaboration with non-Catholic Christians, even in the area of evangelization; on dialogue with the non-Catholic Christian religions; on the problems of secularization and secularism; on the lack of religious freedom in the socialist countries; on a more extensive and better use of the mass media in evangelization.

In this appendix I shall endeavor to treat only one of these themes: evangelization and human progress or liberation, or, to put it in better and more theological terms, *the relation between the eschatological character of Christian salvation and man's progress in time.* In other words, in what sense and to what extent man's purely temporal or earthly progress ("liberation") effects, or becomes part of, the redemption or salvation or sanctification that has been given us by Christ and in Christ. And, consequently, in what sense or in what measure such human progress is part of the Church's duty insofar as she continues the work of Christ and is called upon to evangelize all of mankind. Or, to put it still another way, if one engages in evangelization without also being concerned with or committed to action in behalf of human progress ("liberation"), is one substantially unfaithful to the mission Christ has given to his Church? Does work for liberation (in the social, economic, and political areas) belong to the mission proper of the Church?

This was certainly one of the most important questions discussed at the Synod, and it represents beyond any doubt the great present-day theological problem in Latin America. For this reason, the work of the Synod may perhaps be of help in our Latin American theological discussion.

After I had carefully analyzed all the documentation of the 1974 Synod[4] I decided to present the results in a systematic manner; to present them analytically, according to each document or group of documents, would have been an excessively long process and wearying to the reader. I have taken as my guide the chief statements in the final declaration of the synodal Fathers. The section of the declaration that deals with our themes is number 12, which runs as follows:

> Among the many subjects dealt with by the Synod, special attention was drawn to the mutual relationship between evangelization and integral salvation or the complete liberation of men and of peoples.
>
> In a matter of such importance we experienced profound unity in reaffirming the intimate connection between evangelization and this liberation. We were stimulated to do so not only by close relations with our faithful and with other people, whose life and common fate we share, but primarily by the Gospel mercifully entrusted to us, which constitutes the good news of salvation for all men and for the whole of society. That good news is to be initiated and made manifest on earth from now on, although it is only beyond the confines of this present life that it can achieve its complete fulfillment.
>
> Prompted by the love of Christ and illuminated by the light of the Gospel, let us nurture the hope that the Church, in more faithfully fulfilling the work of evangelization, will proclaim man's total salvation — or rather his complete liberation — and will from now on begin to bring this about. As a community totally involved in evangelization, the Church must, in fact, conform to Christ, who explained His own mission in these words: "The Spirit of the Lord is upon me because he has anointed me; to bring good news to the poor he has sent me, to proclaim to the captives release, and sight to the blind; to set at liberty the oppressed."
>
> Faithful to her evangelizing mission, the Church as a truly poor, praying and fraternal community can do much to bring about the integral salvation or full liberation of men. She can draw

> from the Gospel the most profound reasons and ever new incentives to promote generous dedication to the service of all men — especially the poor, weak and oppressed — and to eliminate the social consequences of sin which are translated into unjust social and political structures. Above all, the Church, supported by Christ's Gospel and fortified by His grace, can harness such dedication for the elimination of deviations. And so the Church does not remain within merely political, social and economic limits (elements which she must certainly take into account) but leads toward freedom under all its forms — liberation from sin, from individual or collective selfishness — and full communion with God and with men as brothers. In this way the Church, in her evangelical way, promotes the true and complete liberation of all men, groups and peoples.[5]

It is easy to see that this passage is more rhetorical than theological or systematic. It mirrors some concerns of the Synod, but the total documentation of the meeting would have allowed, and even urged, that much more should be said. The final text is a thin one. It lacks spirit, decisiveness, and clarity precisely on the points on which clarifications and greater thoroughness were to be expected. Its terminology is confused and ambiguous: salvation, integral salvation, liberation, complete liberation, complete liberation of all men, groups, peoples, full communion with men. In this, as in other points, hasty redaction and improvisation are evident; everything had to be done in practically one day, and by a group gathered for the purpose on that same day; they had no opportunity to study the vast documentation in their possession. Even the emendations (*modi*: suggestions for correction) proposed by many of the synodal Fathers at the last minute were not studied (in some cases not even read), much less profitably used for the improvement of the text. There simply was not enough time. An effort was made to produce at least something, and this something is what has been officially given to us.

In this appendix we shall consider (1) how the Synod of 1974 saw the problem of the relations between evangelization and liberation, (2) the deviations the Fathers saw in the efforts at liberation that are now being made, (3) the meaning of the "intimate connection" between evangelization and human progress, and (4) clarifications offered by the Fathers for the concepts of salvation and liberation.

1. The Problem

Ever since the Second Vatican Council's *Pastoral Constitution on the Church in the Modern World (Gaudium et spes)* and especially since Paul VI's encyclical on the progress of peoples *(Populorum progressio)*, a new, or at least not very traditional, way of looking at things has been widespread in the Church: the duty Christians have of contributing to justice and human progress is now seen, not from the viewpoint of an ethic elaborated solely by human reason, but, first and foremost, in the light of Gospel revelation.[6] The new perspective found its full expression in the "Justice in the World" statement that was produced by the Synod of 1971, especially when, at the end of the Introduction, the Fathers said: "Action on behalf of justice and participation in the transformation of the world clearly appear to us as an essential dimension of the preaching of the Gospel — or in other words, of the Church's mission for the redemption of the human race."[7]

This peremptory statement by the Synod of 1971 inevitably attracted attention; it greatly influenced the discussion at the Synod of 1974. If taken seriously, it cannot but have important repercussions on the work of evangelization (the theme of the 1974 Synod) and the definition of the Church's specific mission. For this reason, not everyone was ready to accept it without further discussion and clarification. The Commission for Justice and Peace, in the document it prepared for the Synod's use, said: "We fervently hope that the Synod of 1974 will devote a great deal of attention to these basic questions in its discussions and declarations." The report of the synodal secretariat on the responses received from the various episcopal conferences shows that many of them hoped to receive from the Synod some clarification of the concept of salvation and its relationship to human progress or liberation. Such a request was specifically made by the episcopal conferences of Belgium, Brazil, Chile, Cuba, Italy, Peru, Poland, Spain, Uganda, Venezuela, and Yugoslavia.

When Pope Paul VI, in his opening address, came to speak of the "specifically religious aim of evangelization," he recognized the objective difficulties those engaged in the apostolate must encounter because the relationship between evangelization and human progress has been obscured: "Very often today they [those in the apostolate] are urged to forget the necessary priority of the salvation message and to restrict their own efforts to mere philanthropic, sociological or political activity, and the scope of the Church to a man-centered, temporal message." He told the Fathers that for this reason "it will be necessary to define more accurately the relationship between evangelization properly so called and the whole human effort toward development, for which the Church's help is rightly expected even though this is not its specific task."[8]

We find the same concern in the various introductory reports. At the request of the Pope, Cardinal Aloisio Lorscheider, president of the Brazilian episcopal conference, redacted a *Panorama* of the general situation of the Church since the Synod of 1971; he composed it after consulting with the episcopal conferences throughout the world. In his report he says that the question of the relations between evangelization and human progress is being raised today "in an often violent manner" (no. 24). He emphasizes, therefore, the pressing need of devoting a great deal of thought to the subject, "taking into account the studies done in recent years on the history of salvation, eschatology, and the various political theologies, as well as on progress and liberation." Cardinal Cordeiro, in his report on Asia, where there is a great deal of poverty and injustice, said that on that continent the need was felt of action in behalf of human progress, but also that there was obscurity on what the relations between evangelization and human progress are or should be; for this reason, some of the Asian episcopal conferences were asking the Synod for a clear statement of principles. Bishop James Sangu, reporting on Africa, declared that to the Africans the question was of "surpassing importance."

It can be said, in the words of Cardinal Marty of Paris, that "all the problems which have a practical effect on evangelization can be summed up in a few words: How are we to conceive the relationship between human liberation and Christian salvation."[9] Cardinal Ribeiro of Lisbon likewise insisted that the question is "burningly topical" and is being raised "on all sides, but especially in the developing nations." Bishop Bernardin, speaking from the viewpoint of a developed nation (the United States), saw in the connection between evangelization and progress "a complex and profound theological problem," and he called attention to the divergence in the situations of "the three worlds" but also, and above all, to the interdependence of these three worlds.

The problem is not completely new, but it is felt more acutely in our day. Contemporary men, especially the young, are increasingly sensitive to unjust situations. This is, as it were, a sign of the present times. In the last century there was a special sensitivity to freedom; in this century there is a great sensitivity to justice. This sign of the times is accompanied by another: contemporary man feels an instinctive and growing distrust of every purely doctrinal message of human liberation, and he measures the value of such messages in terms of their efficacity in really liberating man; in short, he asserts the primacy of praxis. Praxis and orthopraxis are now the criterion for evaluating doctrinal messages. Contemporary man believes more in deeds than in doctrines.[10]

In this situation, effective commitment to liberation will be the most necessary sign of credibility for the Church in today's world. Unless the Church shows a special interest and makes an active and efficacious commitment in this area, she cannot expect to be found credible by our contemporaries. Many of the synodal

Fathers emphasized this point, as, for example, Cardinal Paulo E. Arns of Säo Paulo and Bishop Ramón Torrella, vice-president of the Commission for Justice and Peace. In the document it addressed to the Synod, this commission said: "The present world situation as seen in the light of faith bids us return to the heart of the Christian message and convince ourselves of its true meaning and pressing demands. The mission of preaching the Gospel in our time requires that we commit ourselves to the full liberation of man even now in his earthly life."[11]

The same view was reflected in the pre-synodal report of the Spanish episcopate: "A Christian community in our day cannot beget new children of God through evangelization unless in giving witness to its faith in Jesus Christ it also gives witness to a fraternal love which finds expression as a demand for social justice." French Group B (II) said the same thing: "If it is not to be stripped of its credibility, evangelization must respond to contemporary man's increasing awareness of and sensitivity to the values of justice, peace, and solidarity."[12]

It is clear that this demand for credibility (a concern that is in itself both merited and biblical) simply raises the problem of the relations between evangelization and human progress or liberation; it does not solve this problem. For if a commitment to progress were required solely as a way of achieving credibility, the problem would be one of the politics or tactics of evangelization, not a theological problem raised by revelation.

In any case, the final declaration of the Synod could say very truthfully that "among the many subjects dealt with by the Synod, special attention was drawn to the mutual relationship between evangelization and integral salvation or the complete liberation of men and peoples."

The precise nature of this relationship is the theological problem we wish to discuss in this appendix.

2. Deviations in the Efforts at Liberation

In the final declaration, the Fathers refer to "deviations" that must be eliminated from efforts undertaken for liberation. Many of the pre-synodal and synodal statements showed a rather extensive preoccupation with real or possible deviations, errors, or temptations when it comes to establishing relations between the proclamation of Christian salvation and the effort to promote human progress or man's liberation within time.

Not all talk of liberation is automatically Christian. Speaking shortly after the Synod, on November 3, 1974, Pope Paul VI pointed out that the word liberation is open to divergent and ambiguous interpretations.[13] All the modern forms of humanism (socialism, Marxism, psychoanalysis, secularism, etc.) claim to be liberating, and all denounce various forms of "alienation." Honesty requires the clear-eyed admission that un-Christian and even anti-Christian humanisms exist. It is true, of course, that "nothing genuinely human fails to raise an echo in their [the followers of Christ] hearts" (*GS*, 1/200), but Christianity is nonetheless not a humanism. Or, to express it better, Christian humanism is not purely immanent, locked up in itself.

For the Christian, who believes in a God unlike the god of the deists, a God who is indeed transcendent but who is also immanent, the history of the world and mankind, and especially the history of salvation and the Church, is not a closed system. The factors which explain its development, the reasons for its existence, the finality that governs it, are not purely immanent; that is, they are not found exclusively within this history itself. The acknowledgment that nontheological or purely pragmatic factors (often sociological, psychological, and historical) play a sometimes decisive role should not make us forget other factors which are equally decisive but purely theological and, as such, elude the perception and analysis of the historian, the sociologist, the psychologist, and even the exegete and are perceived solely by faith and in the light of faith.

God calls man to be the master and king of creation, but man is not therefore his own end or the sole or principal artificer and creator of his own history. His history is shaped also by the unforeseeable action of the transcendent God, the Lord of history, and by the fact that this history is oriented toward the eschaton. It is only with this "eschatological proviso" constantly in mind that the Christian can involve himself in history, sociology, or psychology. The Church is at the same time immanent (and as such enters "into the history of mankind" [*LG*, 9g/26]) and transcendent (and as such "transcends all limits of time and of race" [ibid.]).

The Gospel, too, may never be cut off from history and the sociological and psychological conditioning which history makes inevitable. This does not mean, however, that the Gospel is simply a datum for the historian, the sociologist, and the psychologist, or that it can be exhaustively judged by the human sciences, no matter how scrupulously they may approach the subject. Consequently, in studying the Gospel and its essential requirements we should indeed call upon the help of the historians, the sociologists, the psychologists, the exegetes, and the students of the other "human sciences." Yet it is not for these scientists and scholars, as such, to say the final, much less the decisive, word. That word belongs to those who live the Gospel and believe in the word; it belongs to the humble and the lowly, to whom alone the Father reveals the mysteries of his kingdom (cf. Mt 11:25–26). From the others, the "learned and clever" — unless they be also humble men of faith — these realities are hidden by the Father; it is not given to them to know the mysteries of the kingdom of heaven (cf. Mt 13:11).

The Gospel (or, concretely, the Church, whose nature is mysterious is always a mystery made flesh, a whole that contains the divine and the human, the invisible and the visible. These disparate elements are so closely interrelated, so interdependent, that the human and visible always exists in function of the divine and invisible, and draws from the latter the very reason for its being.

At the same time, the divine and invisible expresses itself through the human and visible, and derives from the latter its concrete forms of existence. We can distinguish the two, but we cannot separate them. Any effort to confuse or identify them is an effort to deny them; every effort to divide them and to create a dichotomy or dualism is an effort to destroy them. By themselves and without theology, the human sciences (sociology, economics, politics, psychology, etc.) can never understand or encompass the totality which is the Church; they must be complemented by theology, that is, by "faith seeking understanding." On the other hand, a pure theology that is unaided by the human sciences is always likely to succumb to a contemplative speculation that lacks any realistic bearings and ends in narrow ecclesiasticism and fanaticism.

Wherever this encounter of the divine and the human has taken place in history it has, since the very beginnings of Christianity, been followed by the twofold temptation of identification (monism or monophysitism, in its various forms) or dichotomization (dualism, which also takes many forms). There is always "distinction" or "duality" between the divine and the human, but never "division" or "dualism."

If we are to believe what many of the synodal Fathers tell us, the two temptations of identification and dichotomization are felt today in evangelization and progress. In his official report on Latin America, Bishop Pironio said: "In Latin America, too, there is the danger of a superficial identification of evangelization with human progress; liberation is thus limited to the sphere of the socio-economic and political, or is restricted to the temporal order" (no. 13). Spanish-Portuguese Group B (I) pointed out the temptation "to let the Christian commitment be completely absorbed by its temporal and political dimension, this being regarded as a necessary first stage in every proclamation of the Gospel and the mystery of salvation."

Cardinal Jubany, archbishop of Barcelona, summed up the viewpoint of a lengthy and very rich pre-synodal report of the Spanish episcopate when he denounced the "temporalism" of "minority groups that are nonetheless very influential." It will be worth our while to read the description the Spanish bishops give of this "temporalist" tendency:

> Those who adopt this view start with the postulate that mankind is divided into two groups: the oppressors and the oppressed; they lay the blame for this state of affairs on the existing socio-economic structures which capitalism has created. There can be no encounter of men with the Christ of faith except through an encounter with the oppressed. The Church, for its part, because of the commitments in which it has involved itself through the centuries of its history, is now a barrier that prevents men from taking the side of the oppressed, since the substantial bond that binds the latter together is their commitment to use revolution as the means of ridding the world of oppression. The conclusion drawn is that the "institutional Church" must either be abandoned as a place for encounter with the oppressed brothers or else must be radically transformed.
>
> In this view, the Christ of faith is replaced by the oppressed brother. Any reference to the Christ of faith that is not reducible to a reference to the oppressed brother is suspected of promoting religious alienation. Over against the "official," the "institutional Church," which has been corrupted by its complicity with the ruling classes, a "new Church" is arising: the brotherhood of the oppressed whose real bond is a shared, effective commitment to eliminate oppression from the world.
>
> In such a perspective, the Eucharist too acquires a new meaning. Our present Eucharistic assemblies (these people say) lack Christian meaning. The Eucharist is meant to be the visible sign of loving unity among Christians, but in our churches oppressors and oppressed are to be found in the same congregation. To go on with our present celebrations under such circumstances can only serve to foster the good conscience of the oppressors and to hide oppression under a veil of selfish religious sentiments. The Eucharist will be authentic when it is the Eucharist of the oppressed who are strong in unity and solidarity.
>
> The biblical concept of people is gradually being transformed

into a vague sociological concept. The Gospel is demythologized by means of a political re-reading of it, and is being reduced to the proclamation of a social liberation. Faith loses its explicit reference to Christ and is equated with a commitment to the political liberation of oppressed individuals and peoples.

In this view, the exploitation of men by their fellow men, which is an inevitable consequence of the capitalist organization of society and the economy, is the root of all moral disorders and injustices. Scientific socialism, on the other hand, provides an objective vision of historical events. When the working class is taken up into the communist party, it acquires the strength needed for effecting the social revolution that is an essential requirement if we are to have a truly new human race. A direct evangelization of the oppressed and especially of the working class would be ineffective and antichristian; some disciples might be won, but at the cost of infidelity to the direction of history, which has condemned capitalism beyond hope of forgiveness. Revolution, which is a necessary condition for the integral human development of the oppressed, must precede evangelization. And since the socialist revolution is the change required by science if the present world is to be transformed into a world that respects the dignity of man, the Christian must collaborate in a positive way with the forces of socialism and thus hasten the triumph of the revolution.

That is how the Spanish episcopate analyzes the temporalist tendency.

Bishop Sangu, in his official report on Africa, likewise vigorously denounced a radical *dichotomy* between evangelization and human progress, according to which the Church must first work for progress and only then for evangelization. "We reject the 'modern theology' that says the African Church must first undertake and carry through the worldly development of peoples and only then evangelize them in the proper sense." "It is false and erroneous," he said, "to separate these two tasks."

In its pre-synodal statement (no. 65), the Italian episcopate, too, spoke of Christians ("few in number") who claim that the Church's essential and primary mission in our day is "the liberation of the poor." Some of these Christians reduce evangelization to this kind of liberation; others assert that the Church must first liberate the poor and then evangelize them.[14] According to the Italian bishops, this is in our day "the most crucial and debated problem among Catholics, and a cause of serious divisions in the Church." They insist that the Synod must therefore shed light on the matter.

It would be tiring to list all the synodal Fathers who spoke out against the temporalist trend in its monist or dualist form. But the importance of the document requires that we cite a bit of Cardinal Lorscheider's *Panorama.* Drawing on the reports of the episcopal conferences of the entire world, the president of the Brazilian Episcopal Conference says that the priesthood is now witnessing the rise of a "third man of the Church" (*tertius homo Ecclesiae*). He describes him thus:

> He is unwilling to abandon either the ministry or the faith, although he pays little attention to the life and activity of the Church. On the other hand, he claims to carry out his mission through a "commitment to the poor" and "the oppressed" outside the institutional Church. He remains in the Church in order to "raise the consciousness" of men until a reform of social structures is effected. He cherishes the hope that when these social structures have been destroyed, a "reform" of ecclesiastical structures and the birth of a "new Church" will follow.

Clearly connected with this trend is the tendency to *politicize the faith,* which a number of Latin American bishops point out. Bishop Pironio says in his report (no. 16):

> A superficial politicization of the faith, a crisis of faith arises (when faith is identified in a superfical way with politics), because of the discovery that the Gospel message has a historical dimension and that faith is involved in life. The originality of the Gospel and the truthful testimony of holiness in the Church lose their power. Es-

sential values of prayer and suffering are replaced by the struggle for justice, political action, and even violence.

Spanish-Portuguese Group B (I) spoke of a comparable temptation, that of "taking as the fundamental criterion of the Church's action a political effectiveness that pushes aside and replaces the need of explicitly proclaiming the Gospel in its entirety." Bishop Alfonso López, secretary general of the Latin American Episcopal Conference, made this point: "The 'praxis' of the Church, of which they speak, seems reducible to a political praxis that is exalted into a new transcendental and that will, through the action chiefly of priests, transform that alienating institution, the Church, into a sign of revolutionary commitment, this last being the proof of authentic Christianity."

All these points may be illustrated by the experience of Chile. Bishop Valdés Subercaseaux, bishop of Osorno, described this experience to the synodal Fathers in these terms:

> The only thing regarded as important was to dedicate oneself exclusively to the temporal order. Any sense of the transcendence of God or the Church was pushed almost entirely into the background, while attention was focused almost exclusively on social progress as measured by secular norms. Specialized Catholic action gradually turned into temporal action, since Christians felt a more urgent need of giving themselves to this kind of action; finally, they simply threw themselves directly into political action under the guidance of the various parties, and ended up absorbing political principles rather than those of the Gospel. In vain did individual bishops, and frequently the episcopate as a whole, urge them to avoid errors; the bishops were careful not to break off communication. Most of the "priests for socialism" were foreigners, and propagated their ideas very ably and in quite subtle ways.

It is only a step to what Castillo Lara, auxiliary bishop of Trujillo, Venezuela, called a *naive symbiosis with Marxism*. Spanish-Portuguese Group B (I) likewise called attention to

> the temptation to take over the whole of Marxist doctrine as a conceptual and practical tool which is judged indispensable in analyzing society and effecting needed social change. In so doing, [these Christians] tend to "ideologize" the faith by turning it into a vision of the universe which is in fact contradictory to the faith in its fundamentals, and which progressively eats away at Christian identity, finally leaving only a shell behind. Christian identity is replaced by a messianism that is no longer an authentic Christian eschatology.

French Group B (I) also saw a "danger of temporal messianism."

Again, however, it was Cardinal Jubany, archbishop of Barcelona, who most explicitly pointed out the Marxist tendency "of various Christian groups, clergy, and intellectuals." These people, he explained, choose a miliant Marxism and try to reconcile it with the Christian faith. They argue that Marxism is a method for scientifically analyzing social and political reality; that it has enabled us to see how the mechanisms of oppression proper to the capitalist system actually function, and how a scientifically based social change is possible; and that it enables us to elaborate an overall alternative to capitalism. By taking over Marxism, then, their faith, hope, and love acquire a political dimension and demand a radical change in society. The option for socialism thus flows from the scientific analysis of the contemporary political reality, since the latter shows that Marxist socialism is the only effective way of escaping the contradictions inherent in capitalism. The Marxist Christian is helped in his task by reading the Gospel in the light of his revolutionary political commitment. When all become the criteria for interpreting the Christian message of salvation.

Pope Paul VI certainly had some very specific temptation in mind when, shortly after the Synod, on November 3, 1974, he urged the Latin American bishops to intensify their apostolic efforts and "counteract the temptation, which some feel at times, of embracing ideologies that are alien to the Christian spirit."[15]

French Group B (I) called attention to another danger in this area, that of seeking to please public opinion. In a former age, the temptation was to commit the Church to the established powers. Today, the temptation is to commit the Church to the power of public opinion, although the rule of public opinion is just as dangerous as the dictatorships of the right or the left.

There is also, however, the error of "the insensitivity of some Christians to situations of injustice," as Pope Paul VI called it in his abovementioned address to the Latin American bishops. Cardinal Höffner, archbishop of Cologne, spoke of a "fatalistic quietism" that is resigned to social scandals and is not interested in creating a new social order; such quietism, he said, "is unchristian." Bishop Schmitz, auxiliary bishop of Lima, granted that some people reduce the Gospel to a political and social doctrine (these people are "often impelled by great, even if imprudent, generosity"). But, he told the synodal Fathers, we must ask ourselves honestly: Are such people solely responsible for the tensions now afflicting the Church? Are not they also to blame who fail for other reasons, such as passivity, inertia, or a negative attitude to dialogue? And what of those who refuse to accept and put into practice the spirit and conclusions of the Second Vatican Council and, in Latin America, of the General Conference of the Latin American Episcopate at Medellín? Rivera Damas, auxiliary bishop of San Salvador, felt obliged to admit that "in San Salvador there is perhaps still no awareness of the connection between human liberation and progress, on the one hand, and evangelization, on the other. The reason for this is that the ecclesiology and Christology of Vatican II, with all their implications, have still not been accepted." Perhaps all the bishops of the Synod did not have the courage to make such a public confession.

On this point, once again, Cardinal Jubany came out most explicitly in denouncing a *spiritualist* or dualist *tendency* "that is very widespread among the Catholics of Spain." He listed some of the characteristics of this tendency: the kingdom of God is viewed as an entirely transcendent reality that has no explicit connection with the problems of human society; the specifically Christian life should therefore continue to be a matter solely of worship and individual morality. Christians should be preoccupied with "living in grace," but should not go into the implications of such a life for the temporal order; Catholic Action in the world should be directed solely to individuals (with a view to having them act according to their own consciences), not to institutions, groups, or structures. The social, political, and economic problems of society are purely technical in nature, and must be resolved by individuals; the sphere of influence proper to Christian morality is married life, the family, professional work insofar as it is a witness to a Christian life, and the practice of caritative works. The end result of such an oultook is a rigid dualism between evangelization and human progress.

There must, then, be no dualistic separation, either leftist or rightist; no monistic identification and no opposition; no temporalism and no spiritualism; no social insensitivity and no fatalistic quietism; no reduction of the Gospel to human progress and no reduction of progress to the Gospel. Pope Paul VI put it as follows in his opening address to the Synod: "There is not opposition or separation . . . but a complementary relationship between evangelization and human progress. While distinct and subordinate, one to the other, they converge toward the same end, the salvation of man."[16] He made the point again in his closing discourse: "It [the Synod] has clarified the distinction and complementarity between human progress and the preaching of the mystery of Christ, and has shown how the former must be subordinate to the latter."[17]

There is still need, however, of shedding light on the nature of the relationship between evangelization and human progress, and of showing whether the relationship is extrinsic or intrinsic.

3. An "Intimate Connection"

The final declaration of the Synod states: "In a matter of such importance we experienced profound unity in reaffirming the intimate connection between evangelization and this liberation [i.e., the complete liberation of men and of peoples]."

The declaration is evidently alluding to the statement made by the synodal Fathers in 1971, when they said that action in behalf of justice and participation in the transformation of the world clearly appeared to them to be an "essential dimension" of evangelization.

We can easily see that the statement of 1974 is less strong than that of 1971. "Essential dimension," a very firm and straightforward expression, has been replaced by the vague "intimate connection," which is ambiguous, since it can mean a great deal (an intrinsic, integral, or essential connection) or very little (an extrinsic connection or even one that is only occasional, for example in our day, when it is needed as a sign of credibility). The working paper produced prior to the Synod by the secretariat of the Synod had spoken of an "intimate union" (*intime coniungitur*) between evangelization and human progress. By way of explanation, the paper said that Christian salvation "usually requires some human progress." The words "intimate connection," then, were apparently understood in a rather minimalist sense, with the connection hardly being intrinsic and much less an essential dimension. Our impression is that the "intimate connection" of the final declaration completely ignores the very informative discussion at the Synod and reverts to the pre-synodal working paper.

Some of the opinions were vague or negative, but they were few. Cardinal Bengsch of Berlin ("Second World"), for example, insisted that liberation from political and social oppression is in no sense an integral part of evangelization. His argument in support of this position was that Christ did nothing to liberate the chosen people from the Romans, although the Apostles were very desirous that he should. The kingdom of God, said the cardinal, is purely and solely eschatological. Cardinal González Martin, archbishop of Toledo, who also spoke in the name of other Spanish bishops, likewise thought it an exaggeration to say that human progress and earthly liberation are a constitutive part of evangelization. In his view, these things are rather an "extra measure" or consequence of salvation. Others agreed, and saw action in behalf of progress or liberation as a consequence, an effect, or a fruit of redemption (Cardinal Raimondi), and, in the last analysis, an extrinsic dimension of evangelization.

To this same category, which we can call "extrinsicism," belong those who accepted or called for commitment to liberation solely as a support for Christian witness or as a sign of credibility in a world that is now so concerned with justice. Here, too, we can locate those who asserted the necessity of human progress only as "a work of Christian charity," "a fruit of love," "a sign of charity," or "a work of supererogation," and those who regarded the relations between evangelization and human progress as purely "diplomatic" and taking the form either of a "concordat" or of "separation," brutal or cordial as the case might be.

The general tone of the synodal discussion, however, was much more positive. Under the influence of the synodal statement of 1971, many asserted without qualification that human progress or liberation is a "constitutive dimension" of evangelization. Some, however, asked for an explanation of the exact meaning of these words. The explanation was given by Bishop Ramón Torrella Cascante, who at the Synod of 1971 had been special secretary for dealing with the theme of justice in the world. He explained that the words *ratio constitutiva* meant "integral part"; this, he said, was the authentic meaning attributed to the words by the synodal Fathers in 1971. He added: "They did not mean to say 'essential part,' or at least it is not evident that they meant to do so." The pre-synodal document for the 1974 Synod, submitted by the Commission for Justice and Peace (of which Bishop Torrella was president), gave this further explanation: "Such action is a 'constitutive dimension,' not the 'only' dimension, as though all evangelization had to take the form of action in behalf of justice."

Given these explanations, the statement that "the earthly liberation of man is an integral part of evangelization" is the one that best represents the Synod of 1974. This statement was used by Cardinal Cordeiro in his closing report on part I; by Cardinal Wojtyla in his introductory report on part II; by Cardinal Rosales, archbishop of Cebu; Bishop Angelo Fernandes, archbishop of Calcutta; Bishop Kabangu, bishop of Luebo; and others. In his concluding report, Cardinal Cordeiro explained that the question is not whether evangelization or progress is to be chosen, or which of the two is to be given priority. The Church accepts both as integral parts of her mission; one calls for the other, as the word calls for the deed and the preaching of the word calls for the testimony of a life. The priority given to one or the other will depend on specific situations and circumstances. In his opening report, Cardinal Wojtyla emphasized that eternal salvation and human progress cannot be separated in the action of the Church or of any Christian, since the two are intimately united as parts of the one work of creation and redemption.

For the same reasons, others spoke of a "necessary bond" or a "necessary link" between the two — for example, Bishop Matagrin of Grenoble, speaking in the name of the French episcopate, in an excellent address to which we must return below. French Group B (I) likewise said that evangelization "necessarily" includes the proclamation of economic and social liberation; the group (joined by Bishop Helder Cámara) insisted that "the peaceful struggle for liberation is a Christian duty." The Spanish-Portuguese Group (II) stated it well when it said that "evangelization is not reducible to human progress but it does include such progress, calls for it, and brings it to its perfection"; this group drew its words from the address of Cardinal Jubany, archbishop of Barcelona and spokesman for the majority of the Spanish episcopate.

In their pre-synodal report, the Brazilian bishops had already said that "human progress and evangelization are two aspects of a single comprehensive reality, and not distinct realities or activities" (proposition 92). One reality with two aspects also sums up the position maintained at the Synod by Cardinal Arns, archbishop of Säo Paulo: authentic evangelization includes human progress, and authentic, integral human progress includes evangelization. Bishop Tzadua of Addis Ababa expressed a quite similar thought. Finally, Spanish-Portuguese Group A (II) presented a lengthy statement on the "real and intrinsic relation" between evangelization and human progress. They, says the group, are not to be confused or identified, but neither are they to be regarded as completely independent activities, for "to a Christian, religion is not a narrowly defined area that is cut off from the rest of human life and activity."

Others, however, wanted even more than this. Some, such as Germán Schmitz, auxiliary bishop of Lima and the most active of the synodal Fathers, or Father Goossens, from among the religious superiors general, spoke unreservedly of earthly human liberation (in a sense that will later have to be analyzed in a more nuanced fashion) as an "essential part" of evangelization. Cardinal Conway, archbishop of Armagh, offered a correction: "essential, but subordinate."

It was against this background that the "Statement on Human Rights and Reconciliation," which was sponsored by Cardinals Arns and Krol, approved by Pope Paul VI, and officially issued on October 10, 1974, could say: "In our time the Church has grown more deeply aware of this truth [that the integral development of persons is a manifestation of the divine image in them]; hence she firmly believes that the promotion of human rights is required by the Gospel and is *central to her ministry.*"[18]

Given this divergence of views, we must grant that it is impossible to define in some one and exclusive manner the relations between eschatological salvation and man's progress on earth. A number of the responses submitted by the episcopal conferences before the Synod called attention to the variety of situations with which the Church must deal. In view of this variety, in which some situations show more wretchedness and injustice than others, there will also be different responses to the task of liberation; diversity of circumstances will determine how pastors see the link between liberation and evangelization, and the importance they assign to liberation within the overall work of evangelization. Everything will depend on the circumstances of time and place: in one situation, the very possession of goods in abundance hinders evangelization and makes it difficult; in another, the lack of material things will place obstacles in the way of pastoral action.

Cardinal Cordeiro, in his concluding report on the first part of the discussion, emphasized this diversity of situation when he said that

> in places where millions of men are living wretched lives as victims of injustice and oppression, action geared to human advancement and liberation will be a necessary part of evangelization. In these situations the Church is obliged to stand by the poor and oppressed, to carry on her prophetic role, and to help change structures and the outlook of people.

The first draft of a final document (which was, however, rejected as a whole in a preliminary vote on October 22, 1974) stated that "a commitment to liberation and the building of the world is an integral part of salvation and evangelization." In support of this assertion, the text argued that positive zeal for a better world is not simply a fruit of charity or a motive of credibility but a good thing *in itself* (words italicized in the draft). The draft added, however, that such a commitment to liberation is "not an essential part of salvation" and must therefore always be a relative thing, since it will be called for by the weakness that is part of human nature. Faith does not eliminate this weakness, but it bestows a new value on suffering and difficulties by making them a means of salvation, as is indicated in the old adage

Per crucem ad lucem (Through the cross to the light). We must therefore acknowledge that evangelization will always be necessary and difficult, even in a world not marked by any great injustice and inequality.

Another problem that was frequently raised in this context was *varying responsibilities.* It is easy to say that "the Church" must do this or that. But who or what is this Church? The Synod of 1971 had been aware of this problem. The document *Justice in the World* distinguishes "the Church," "the hierarchy," and "Christians." Christians, "as members of society, have the same right and duty to promote the common good as have other citizens," but "in such activities . . . [they] generally act on their own initiative without involving the responsibility of the ecclesiastical hierarchy."[19]

At the Synod of 1974, Cardinal Poma, archbishop of Bologna, asked for a clearer definition of the responsibilities of the Church as such and those of Christians who must as citizens take part in public life and share the task of promoting progress. Along the same lines, Bishop Moreira Neves, vice-president of the Council for the Laity, emphasized the specific role of the laity in this area. So did Cardinal Gonzáles Martin and Father Agostini, one of the superiors general. The latter, like the others, quoted the words of the Second Vatican Council: "The laity have the principal role in the universal fulfillment of this purpose [i.e., in seeing that "the world is permeated by the spirit of Christ and more effectively achieves its purpose in justice, charity, and peace"]" (*LG*, 36c/62–63). Pope Paul VI said the same in his opening address. Similar views were expressed by several of the discussion groups, for example, the Italian and the English B (I), which said that "the duty of advancing the process of liberation is one that belongs especially to the laity, who must infuse Christian principles into all activities and institutions."

The final declaration of the Synod, nonetheless, speaks only of "the Church" and does not differentiate between responsibilities.

4. Clarification of the Concepts of Salvation and Liberation

A great deal depends on how we understand such words and phrases as salvation, integral salvation, kingdom of God, eschatology, human progress, development, liberation, complete liberation, alienation, sins, roots of sin, consequences of sin, charity, justice, poor, poverty, oppressor, oppressed, dependence, political, political dimension of the faith, privatization of the faith, institutional Church, and so on. We live in an age that is quite hostile to the defining of concepts (to "conceptualism" or "ontologism") but, at the same time, inundates us with words and slogans. This anticonceptual and antiontological feeling has brought a new form of nominalism. There are plenty of words, but what precisely does each one mean? Even the final declaration of the Synod calmly speaks of "integral salvation" and "complete liberation," and three times uses these expressions as synonyms; it seems to suppose that the reader will have an exact grasp of their theological meaning or content.

As a matter of fact, however, these expressions have not been current in theology, and a reader does not know quite what to make of them. In their responses to the working paper that had been prepared by the synodal secretariat, many episcopal conferences complained that the much-used word salvation was never once defined. In its report on these responses, the secretariat in turn complained that neither did the episcopal conferences provide any material for a better or more extensive clarification of the concept of Christian salvation. On the first page of this report we read:

> It is to be observed that the views expressed in the replies [of the episcopal conferences] vary a great deal, so that what some praise others disparage. There seem to be good grounds for the remark that the Church no longer possesses a common language. There is evident need of a dialogue within the Church herself.

The working paper puts its finger on a disturbing fact: *The Church no longer possesses a common language!*

We shall see, nonetheless, that the documents of the Synod provide material which can help in a needed clarification of the concepts of salvation and liberation. With regard to these two concepts, at least, we *do* possess a common language.

Salvation

I think it can be said, without need of proof, that the synodal Fathers were unanimous in the conviction that Christian salvation is not reducible to anything temporal, historical, and earthly or to a mystique of simple human brotherhood. "For the Christian, Christ is something more than an exemplar of moral behavior or a motive for greater generosity to God and men," as the Spanish episcopate put it in the statement it prepared for the Synod.

Here are the points the various synodal documents make in regard to the Christian concept of salvation:

a) *The concept of salvation-liberation differs in the Old Testament and in the New.* The Italian episcopate in its pre-synodal document (nos. 68–70) calls attention to this point. It explains that, in the Old Testament, salvation and liberation are essentially salvation and liberation from the enemies which oppress Israel (Egypt, Assyria, etc.) and that the salvation envisaged is earthly and historical. In the New Testament, however, salvation in its ultimate essence comprises a liberation from sin and death and a life of intimacy with God in which men share his eternal and infinite joy; salvation is thus essentially spiritual and eschatological. We cannot be satisfied with the Old Testament concept, since this, says the Italian Group (II), "is inadequate for conveying the Christian meaning of human progress."

b) On the other hand, it is also clear that the current discussion of liberation brings home to us *the inadequacy of a rather traditional concept of salvation, which is spiritualist and eschatological in character, but lacks a historical and earthly dimension,* and means by "salvation" only "saving the soul." Cardinal Arns of Säo Paulo rightly emphasized the fact that the expression "save one's soul" is dualistic and individualistic; consequently, it does not express the whole truth but, on the contrary, alienates man from himself by locating salvation at the moment of death or after death. We must never forget, however, that this salvation of the soul and the eschatological happiness of man in the vision of God is a very important essential element in salvation and must continue to be a principal component of the concept of salvation, even when salvation is no longer thought of as "purely eschatological."

c) Our Christian concept of salvation contains what many Fathers spoke of as a *specific contribution of the Gospel* (Cardinal Ribeiro of Lisbon), or "the specific character of the Gospel message" or "what is authentically original in Christianity" (Bishop Pironio). In his closing address, Pope Paul VI rightly insisted that

> we must see to it that the real point of the Gospel message is kept unchanged, namely, that God redeems man from sin and death and leads him to participation in the divine life. Consequently, man's temporal and social progress is not to be so emphasized that we lose sight of the essential meaning which the Church gives to evangelization or the preaching of the Gospel in its entirety.[20]

This means we must say clearly that every concept of salvation which does not safeguard this primordial and essential element of the Gospel is ambiguous and un-Christian.

d) It is also necessary, however, to assert that *Christian salvation also has an earthly and historical dimension*. Bishop Schmitz, auxiliary bishop of Lima, pointed out the change that has taken place: formerly, there was a tendency to locate salvation entirely in "the next life" and to preach a resignation which paralyzed men when it came to collaborating in the earthly progress of mankind;[21] today, without forgetting the next life, we also insist on the historical "here and now" as an essential facet of salvation.

Spanish-Portuguese Group C (II) points out that today's Christian must be concerned with "man himself, whole and entire, body and soul, heart and conscience, mind and will" (*GS,* 3b/201), time and eternity. In this sense the Group speaks of "integral salvation," an expression that became synonymous with "complete liberation" in the final declaration of the Synod.

e) We can now see more clearly that concern for human progress is not merely a practical conclusion to be drawn from the experience of evangelization, but an authentic *locus theologicus* (theological source) which requires of the Christian, committed to human progress, an adaptation of his Christian practice to the present age (orthopraxis) and, to this end, a reading of the Gospel from a new point of view. The *hermeneutical value of situations as a theological source* is to some extent a novelty in theology; as is usually the case with novelties, some have carried it to unacceptable lengths. For this reason, it was an object of concern at the Synod and before it.

The Italian bishops saw it as "one of the most difficult problems that has arisen since the Council." The statement which the Latin American episcopal conference prepared for the Synod asks that special attention be given to determining the sense in which the tendencies and aspirations of men are in fact a "theological source." The statement observes that this view has unfortunately been misinterpreted or misapplied at times, with individuals believing that the Bible can be replaced in everyday life by a "revelation through events." We must be on guard lest dependence on existential situations lead us to detract from the integrity of the Gospel message.[22]

The Italian bishops were worried chiefly by the position of those who think that the Gospel and the Church's tradition should be judged by "the signs of the times," and not the reverse. These bishops note that two mysteries are unfolding simultaneously in the course of history: the "mystery of salvation" and the "mystery of iniquity." History is therefore God's word, but a word that reaches man's ears inextricably commingled with other words that are "worldly" or "diabolical." History and events are assuredly a "theological source," but spiritual discernment must be exercised toward them so that we do not take as a word from God what is in fact only a human word or even a word from the evil one (no. 76).

Spanish-Portuguese Group A (II) has some very worthwhile things to say on this point:

> Historical events do not constitute a new revelation. They only contain the historical revelation of Jesus Christ to the extent that they mediate an action of the Holy Spirit. Their entire content is a message concerning the paschal mystery as the latter is actualized today by the Spirit in the ongoing history of mankind. An authentic interpretation of the "signs of the times" supposes the prophetic charism of discernment, and this last must show the essential marks of authentic prophetic activity: intimate participation in the history of mankind and a personal experience of the transcendence of God. The interpretation of the signs of the times is not a purely rational or logical activity, but requires the contemplative outlook of one who lets Jesus Christ take possession of him and who, moved by the Spirit, without reserve embraces the human beings who are his brothers and sisters. The interpretation of the signs is the work of the entire ecclesial community, especially of the bishops who are its pastors; special importance is to be attributed, however, to individuals who are prophets — that is, men of God — who, in and for the community, grasp the deeper meaning of events.
>
> Since the history of mankind is ambiguous from the viewpoint of salvation, wavering as it does between God's rule and the rejection of that rule, the interpretation of the signs of the times is a difficult task that must be approached with humble simplicity. A facile optimism in interpreting the signs can lead to overestimation of the salvific value of history and a kind of "inflation" of the signs by assuming that God's action in history can be expressed in ambiguous events. But God does not manifest himself in ambiguous or negative deeds. It is above all in simple events and realities that he shows himself. In our day we must open our eyes

to the new and truly meaningful events which proclaim the Church's return to essentials: fidelity, prayer, loving contact with our brothers, and a full and integral freedom. Discernment of the signs of the times presupposes that a positive exercise of the Church's teaching authority creates an opening to new ways.

f) These legitimate concerns of the bishops in regard to the hermeneutic value of specific situations should not cause us to minimize the true significance of this "theological source." Bishop Matagrin, spokesman for the French episcopate, put it well when he said that *the present situation is very beneficial for our Christian concept of salvation.* We are now in a position to purify, deepen, and enrich that concept. We see more clearly that salvation is not purely temporal or purely spiritual; it is not merely the forgiveness of sin or an individual reward. We understand better the theological and paschal riches of the concept, which comprises entering into filial communion with the living God, experiencing that we are loved and accompanied in life and in death by the God who raised Christ from the dead, sharing in the fulfillment of God's plan for history, removing all fatalism from human affliction, and entering into the reign of love that originates in the Father. We discover the eschatological and all-embracing nature of salvation, for salvation is the promise of a creation that has been set free and of an unconditioned future for a mankind remade in the image of the risen Christ, so that all of human history acquires a new dimension.

g) The French bishops (in the person, still, of Bishop Matagrin) go on to speak of *the need of justifying the many ties between evangelization and liberation, without, however, indulging in either a facile concordism or a facile reductionism.* They suggest six steps which will enable us to attain a better insight into the links:

1. The Gospel is preached to men, in order that they may freely decide to acknowledge God in Jesus Christ. This means the Church must accept such undertakings as can help human communities

to a responsible commitment and decision concerning their own lives. In other words, a certain degree of liberation is a condition for evangelization.

2. Human efforts at liberation thus provide a context in which revelation can be welcomed and understood in depth (here, again, we meet the idea of the situation as a "theological source").

3. Undertakings in behalf of human liberation draw light and strength from the Gospel. The Gospel can help men (a) discern prophetically the ambiguities attaching to certain undertakings, (b) gain insight into kinds of alienation that lie deeper and are more hidden, (c) criticize the means that are used to liberate men, (d) unmask new forms of idolatry.

4. Activity in behalf of liberation is a privileged ground for the encounter and dialogue of believers and nonbelievers, for in such activity they share the search for a life untouched by fatalism and marked by great aspiration and hope. It will be possible, too, for the Gospel to be shared as the Good News sent by God.

5. Undertakings for the liberation of man from injustice should be regarded by the believer as a means of giving historical proof of his conversion to the Gospel and as an opportunity for allowing faith to produce signs of itself in the "here and now" of human life.

6. The authentic fruits of efforts to liberate men here and now are a sharing by anticipation in the kingdom of God. They can be regarded as part of the final fulfillment brought by Christ, the Lord and Judge of history.

All these points enable us to understand what the Synod means by saying, in its final declaration, that the Church "can draw from the Gospel the most profound reasons and ever new incentives to promote generous dedication to the service of all men."

h) Cardinal Höffner, archbishop of Cologne, who is known for his work on social problems (he had been professor of sociology at the University of Münster), gave the following *reasons why Christians must accept responsibility for human liberation.*

1. It is never legitimate to degrade man by making him a mere object of some governmental, economic, or social process. "The social order and its development must unceasingly work to the benefit of the human person if the disposition of affairs is to be subordinate to the personal realm and not contrariwise" (*GS,* 26c/225).

2. Christ redeemed man in his entirety, which includes his social relationships.

3. Even after original sin, the relationships between men and society which God made part of human nature must be respected.

4. Through his incarnation, the Son of God entered into the history of mankind and the social life of men. If, therefore, the faithful avoid responsibility for society, they sin against the incarnation of the Son of God.[23]

5. The social conditions in which men live are important even for eternal salvation, for it cannot be denied that "men are often diverted from doing good and spurred toward evil by the social circumstances in which they live and are immersed from their birth" (*GS,* 25c/224).

To these reasons I can add others that I heard in the synodal meeting hall:

— Liberation, in the sense of a greater human fulfillment, is part of God's saving plan (Bishop Schmitz, auxiliary bishop of Lima).

— The Church was founded in order to establish the kingdom of God, beginning here on earth.

— There is an essential connection between love of God and love of neighbor, and Christian love cannot be separated from justice (Bishop Torrella); there is an authentic conversion to Christ only when there is also a conversion to love of neighbor, and there is an authentic love of neighbor only when there is a conversion to justice (Spanish-Portuguese Group C [II]).

— Christian salvation and human progress are closely connected in both creation and redemption (Cardinal Wojtyla); human progress is, as it were, the continuation of creation (English Group C [II]).

— The man who has been interiorly freed by Christ will be the greatest force in the construction of history (Cardinal Ribeiro of Lisbon); the chief mission of the Church must therefore be to urge the conversion of the heart, whereby, through the grace of the Spirit, a new man is created in the image of Christ. This conversion does not affect only the private life of the believer, but makes it imperative that the believer commit himself to the transformation of the world in the spirit of the Beatitudes (Spanish-Portuguese Group C [I]). This was the thought of Pope Paul VI in his address to the Latin American bishops on November 3, 1974: "Once man has been interiorly transformed, once he becomes the conscious bearer of the values which faith and grace have engendered in his soul, once the dynamism of love has taken hold of his soul, the sure consequence will be the integral development of a society in which genuine freedom and justice are the basis for all progress."[24]

Liberation

"Liberation" was perhaps the word most often heard at the Synod, and it was on the lips of the representatives from every continent. "'Liberation' is the great password of the day," noted the Italian bishops in their pre-synodal report (no. 16). And Pope Paul VI said, after the Synod, that "liberation" is "a word which the Church holds in high esteem and makes its own, for it meets the word in its own fundamental doctrine of the redemption that liberates man from evil, that is, from sin." But, the Pope added, "as we are all aware, the word 'liberation' can also be given doubtful interpretations."[25]

As a matter of fact, *the word is not always given the same meaning.* It is used by Christians, socialists, Marxists, psychoanalysts, humanists, secularists, atheists, politicians, economists, sociologists, psychologists, philosophers, and theologians, and its meaning differs from group to group. "It is the spiritual tragedy of the modern age," said Bishop Matagrin, "that efforts in behalf of human liberation have often led to a rejection of man's relation to God as being a cause of alienation, and have given rise to Promethean atheism."

Christians were certainly the first to use the word; they took it as a synonym for the redemption effected by Christ. Today, however, not even all Christians who use it give it its biblical, New Testament meaning. Bishop Roa Pérez, archbishop of Maracaibo, Venezuela, observes that in the countries of the Third World "liberation" usually has a political and revolutionary meaning (cf. his emendation to the final declaration of the Synod). In his report on Latin America, Bishop Pironio said that "among us the hope of salvation is often expressed in terms of liberation" (no. 12), but he also admitted that the liberation is at times purely socioeconomic and political in scope.

Nonetheless, the synodal Fathers unanimously agreed that, for a Christian, "liberation cannot depend on political and economic factors alone" (Bishop Tomasek of Prague); that scientific or technological progress is not enough (Spanish episcopate); that liberation will not result simply from changes in structures (Bishop Valdés of Osorno, Chile). As the statement of the Spanish episcopate explained,

> no matter what social reforms or revolutions may be successfully carried through, man will always be a prey to powerful forms of selfishness, both individual and collective; he can make an instrument of oppression out of any and every scientific, economic, cultural, technological, social, or political advance. The root of this possibility is to be found within the very heart of man. Man needs to be radically transformed into a new man.

As the German Group (II) put it, "The world will be radically changed only in the degree that the hearts of men are converted."

On this important point, the Spanish-Portuguese Group (II) said some illuminating things:

> To not a few Christians of our day who are struggling for the social and economic liberation of the poor and the oppressed, economic and social structures that create power and cause oppression are the sole causes of all the evils from which the poor suffer. But it is a fundamental error to think that social inequities originate solely in the tension within economic, political, and social structures, and that once these are changed man will be able to restore a kind of lost paradise. These Christians are certainly right in denouncing oppressive structures and the mechanisms by which some men dominate others, and in claiming that these structures are one cause of structures leading to an unjust dependence, and that, if these structures are removed or destroyed, human life, both individual and social, can and should improve. Nonetheless, Christians committed to the struggle to free man from economic, social, political, and cultural enslavement must not forget that the radical liberation of man, as seen in the light of faith, takes place at the far deeper level of the opening of the heart to God through a conversion (Rom 7:15; Eph 4:19; Gal 3:27).
>
> Even in a different social situation (one that some describe as that of the "new man") a deeper-lying cause of trouble will continue to exist within man himself, a cause that is identical with the human condition itself and therefore is to be found in the human being from the moment of his birth. This cause is man's congenital inclination to evil, which St. Paul describes in Romans 7:13–25 and to which Christ refers in Mark 7:21–23. A Christian and Catholic theology of liberation must always bear in mind that until the second coming of Christ the liberation of man will always be rendered uncertain by the weakness of man and that it is always threatened by the lord of darkness who goes about like a roaring lion, seeking whom he may devour (1 Pt 5:8). It can only be illusion and self-deception to think that the kingdom of God can be fully established here on earth before the parousia. Our Christian hope is eschatological and, as such, differs essentially from the Marxist hope. On the other hand, man's initial redemp-

tion, or liberation and sanctification, though strictly personal and effected by Christ alone, also has a social and even cosmic dimension that is not a mere afterthought but an intrinsic requirement.

Those who want to promote man's liberation must begin by converting themselves, said English Group B (I). And the Latin Group asserted that liberation from political, economic, cultural, and other forms of oppression is impossible if it is not based on the liberation from evil which Christ effected. It is this latter liberation that is the primary content of evangelization.

Perhaps the most valuable contribution to the Christian concept of liberation is to be found in *the distinction between "having more" and "being more."* Many of the addresses and other documents of the 1974 Synod emphasized this distinction, and it is regrettable that it did not find a place in the final declaration, although a number of the offered emendations asked that it should. (Unfortunately, lack of time prevented these emendations even from being read by the commission that was charged with their revision; I myself was part of this commission.) Vatican II had already stated: "A man is more precious for what he is than for what he has" (*GS*, 35b/233). And everyone will recall what Paul VI said in his encyclical *The Progress of Peoples:*

> Today we see men trying to secure a sure food supply, cures for diseases, and steady employment. We see them trying to eliminate every ill, to remove every obstacle which offends man's dignity. They are continually striving to exercise greater personal responsibility; to do more, learn more, and have more so that they might increase their personal worth.[26]

Or again: "Each man can grow in humanity, enhance his personal worth, and perfect himself."[27]

Speaking of charity, the working paper prepared by the synodal secretariat (no. 34) says that charity must not be exercised solely in individual relationships,[28] but also requires communal public efforts to change overall conditions and social and political structures, so that men may not only "have more" but also "be more" and thus be freer. It was in this sense, says the working paper, that the Synod of 1971 declared action in behalf of justice and the transformation of the world an "essential dimension" of evangelization.

In the report with which he introduced the second phase of the discussion, Cardinal Wojtyla said that the progress in question is the progress by which "a man is more precious for what he is than for what he has." In two addresses, Father Goossens, one of the superiors general, likewise strongly emphasized the progress which consists in being more, being better, being a person, and, above all, in promoting "communities of persons." Among his remarks: "Every act that creates a community of persons builds the kingdom of God and the family of God."

However, the person who most systematically bombarded the secretariat with suggestions based on this distinction was Bishop Schmitz, auxiliary bishop of Lima. He, like the other Peruvian representative, Archbishop Durand of Cuzco, insisted on using the term liberation (which he said was better than "development" or "human progress") and distinguishing it from "development."

"Development," he said, has to do with "having more" and can express a "developmentalist" outlook that does not necessarily lead to the advancement of man's dignity as a person. "Liberation" has to do with "being more" and looks to the very core of man's personal dignity, which reaches its highest point when man becomes an adoptive son of God. Liberation, thus conceived, will have as a *consequence* a certain material progress: "Seek first his [God's] kingship over you, his way of holiness, and all these things will be given you besides" (Mt 6:33). Human progress or liberation in the direction of "being more" is part of the very mission of the Church. Progress in the line of "having more" is not a direct part of the Church's mission; it is included in "all these things" that "will be given you besides," provided you "seek *first* his kingship over you, his way of holiness."

This distinction enabled Bishop Schmitz to describe more precisely the relationship between Christian salvation and human progress. If "human progress" is understood solely along the lines of "having more," and if "Christian salvation" is understood solely as a plenitude of divine blessings in eternity, then the relation between the two will be purely extrinsic.

If, however, "human progress" (or, better, "liberation") is understood in terms of "being more," that is, as a process by which man overcomes everything (from the sin that dwells in him to the social effects of sin) that keeps him from being fully a man, then progress, or liberation, and salvation are one and the same reality, viewed from different angles. Liberation will be an *essential part,* though not the whole, of Christian salvation and therefore a direct object of evangelization. Evangelization is precisely the means which will assure that man's liberation is not conceived in a purely immanent manner as a merely political, social, and economic liberation, but will include the more profound and radical liberation from sin and will be open to the full transcendent communion with God as Father and the fraternal communion of men as brothers.

This is the "complete liberation" to which the Synod refers in its final declaration.

These, then, are the data I have derived from the synodal documents on the theme of evangelization and liberation, and these pages have been more a report than a theological study, even if the reporter's thinking or inclinations have shown through at times.

Theological reflection on the data could give a new focus to the theology of liberation. I say this because I think that the Synod of 1974 has clarified some concepts that have to do either with possible deviations (the negative aspect) or with key terms in a theology of liberation (the positive aspect). If, for example, there were to be unanimity in understanding liberation as having to do with "being more," and in integrating liberation, thus understood, with the Christian concept of salvation (so that the two represent "a single reality with two dimensions"), we would have the basis for a new and very valuable way of defining the Church's proper mission and evangelizing task.

Such a theological study would have to go more deeply into the concept of "being more" as it applies to all the dimensions of human nature (Christian anthropology would have specific and quite original contribution to make here). It would be necessary to see how, specifically, such a concept of "being more" could or could not apply to "Latin American man." It would also be necessary to analyze in detail the causes (the general ones, common to all men, beginning with original sin, and those specific to Latin America) which in fact prevent "growth in humanness." Finally, there would have to be a study of "what is to be done" (with special attention to "diversification of responsibilities") in order that the Church may do her duty in helping the process of overcoming everything that keeps man from being fully a man and a Christian.

Notes

1. The transactions of the conference were published under the title *Liberación y Cautiverio* (Mexico City: n.p., 1975). Sobrino's words are on p. 190.

2. This final statement was published in *Medellín* in March 1976 (pp. 144–50), the cited text is from no. 25, pp. 148–49.

3. On the history of the movement, cf. Pablo Richard, *Cristianos por el Socialismo: Historia y documentos* (Salamanca: Sígueme, 1976 [283 pp.]; Teresa Donoso Loero, *Historia de los Cristianos por el Socialismo* (Santiago: Editoria Vaitea, 1976 [209 pp.]; Alfredo Fierro Bardaji and Reyes Mate Rupérez, *Cristianos por el Socialismo: Documentación* (Estella, Navarre: Editorial Verbo Divino, 1975 [498 pp.]; *Cristianos Latinoamericanos y Socialismo* (Bogotá: CEDIAL, 1972 [296 pp.]; Cesar Sanchez-Aiscorbe S.J., "Cristianos por el Socialismo: La discusión en torno al movimiento," *Razón y Fe* (June 1976), pp. 525–39.

The "Bulletin" (in Spanish) of *Liaisons Internationales* (Paris, Centre Oecuménique des Liaisons Internationales) publishes all the documents that come out. "The purpose [of the center] is to gain knowledge of the experiences of Christians throughout the world as they struggle for the liberation of individuals and peoples, and to make others aware of these experiences. Their Churches are often isolated and have no contact with others . . . because they have no media at their disposal and frequently are deliberately ignored by a large sector of the Christian press, which is the voice of the institutional Church" (Bulletin 1 [Aug. 1974]).

4. For a bibliography, cf. Roger Vekemans S.J., *Teología de la liberación y Cristianos por el Socialismo* (Bogotá: CEDIAL, 1976 [592 pp.]).

5. *Liaisons Internationales,* Bulletin 7 (Sept. 1975 [pp. 23ff.]), reports on the CfS movements in Italy, Peru, Venezuela, Holland, Portugal, Switzerland, India, Sri Lanka, Malaysia, Indonesia, Bangladesh, The Philippines, Hong Kong, Thailand, South Korea, Japan, and Vietnam.

6. The document of the First Commission of the Quebec convention says to be converted means "to take one's place in the subversive practice of the poor who accept responsibility for building a new earth" (25/3.1). The final statement of the convention teaches: "To make one's own the

subversive practice of the exploited who are seeking to build a new earth is to have the experience of evangelical conversion and to acquire a new human and Christian identity" (24). Gustavo Gutiérrez, in his *A Theology of Liberation: History, Politics and Salvation* (trans. Sr. Caridad Inda and John Eagleson [Maryknoll, N.Y.: Orbis, 1973]), says: "To be converted is to commit oneself to the process of the liberation of the poor and oppressed" (p. 205). See Pope Paul VI, apostolic exhortation *Evangelii nuntiandi* (Dec. 8, 1975), nos. 18, 19, 36, for a quite different concept of the Christian mission. See also Vatican Council II, *Pastoral Constitution on the Church in the Modern World,* nos. 10, 13, 25.

7. There is enough material on tactics and strategy for a whole, separate study. In July 1973 the CfS of Chile drew up a document, "Agitación y propaganda, comunicaciones y evangelización en CpS" (published in Richard, *op. cit.*, pp. 272–76), according to which CfS aims "to present a Christ who is a liberator, and to link Christianity with the revolution so that the people may feel themselves to be automatically Christian when they are engaged in the struggle." In the section on methodology, the document proposes to establish unchanging symbols and slogans for the masses; to use song, drama, and other artistic means to bring out the causes of the alienation of the people, and the steps the people are taking for their own liberation; to establish a permanent company of CfS actors who will visit the various towns; to publish fliers and pamphlets in which local problems will be related to the overall class struggle; after Mass, to distribute CfS materials that will urge Christians to reflect on their commitment and solidarity; to mount short campaigns within the towns to stimulate discussion of Christian responsibility; to participate, as CfS, in conjunctural situations (neighborhoods, unions, politics) in which the people are advancing toward liberation; when facing problems relative to ecclesiastical institutions and the hierarchy, to establish direct communication with all the regional members and send all information (indicating its degree of confidentiality); to attack reformism and efforts to establish a Christian "third way"; to publish posters, pamphlets, booklets, and books, and to distribute them according to a rational, organized plan.

Commission II of the Chilean convention said: "The people is mobilized by means of unions, parties, seizure of lands, strikes, and student movements" (5/p. 209).

8. This document may be found in Richard, *op. cit.*, pp. 239–41.

9. The identification of the SAL group with the CfS is clear from Bulletin 11 (May 1975) of the SAL group of Medellín. In presenting the Quebec document and the documents of the five commissions at the Quebec convention, the SAL group says: "We have examined this dossier and to our great satisfaction have found that the 'Minimal Consensus,' our recent National Convention, and the other works we are undertaking are in agreement with the documents of the International Convention." On SAL and related movements in Colombia, the Episcopal Conference of

Colombia, at its Thirty-second Plenary Meeting (Nov. 1976), published a rich pastoral statement titled *Identidad cristiana en la acción por la justicia* (Bogotá: SPEC, 1976; 73 pp.).

10. See the letter (Mar. 19, 1973) of Fr. Guillermo Redington of the National Secretariat of CfS at Santiago: "We received word of the formation in February of the Lation American Federation of Priests' Movements (at Lima), under the direction of Gustavo Gutiérrez. Our coordinating committee appointed Gonzalo Arroyo, who is in charge of international CfS relations, as our delegate to the Federation." Cf. Vekemans, *op. cit.*, p. 372.

11. This "Summary of the Minutes" was published in *Contacto* (Mexico City) in December 1973 (pp. 75–80). It is also printed in *Tierra Nueva* (Bogotá), no. 14 (pp. 12–16), with a lengthy commentary by Bishop Alfonso López Trujillo (pp. 17–53).

12. Published in *Liaisons Internationales,* Bulletin 4 (Jan.–Feb. 1975), pp. 11–12.

13. Published in *Liaisons Internationales,* Bulletin 7 (Sept.–Nov. 1975), pp. 32–35.

14. Cf. *Fe cristiana y cambio social en America Latina* (Salamanca: Sígueme, 1973), p. 234.

15. *Op. cit.*, p. 16.

16. "Evangelización y liberación popular," in *Liberación y cautiverio,* pp. 209–33; the quotation is from p. 223.

17. Hugo Assmann, "Iglesia Popular," *Contacto* (Dec. 1975), p. 29.

18. Francisco Vanderhoff and Miguel Angel Campos, "La Iglesia Popular: Condiciones político-ideológicas para su surgimiento," *Contacto* (Dec. 1975). Cf. also *Liberación y cautiverio,* p. 287.

19. In other words, it is not enough for people to be little and lowly (cf. Mt 11:25). There is no contradiction, however, between being not-poor and being humble. It is certainly not God's will that man should live in material poverty or oppression or sickness. Therefore, to live in a situation of nonpoverty is a Christian ideal and perfectly compatible with the other Christian ideal, which is to hear and understand the word of God.

20. Cf. Alfredo Fierro, *The Militant Gospel: A Critical Introduction to the Political Theologies,* trans. John Drury (Maryknoll, N. Y.: Orbis, 1977). The author asks: "What will happen when oppression disappears and there are no more people to liberate? For we must assume that liberation theology aspires to the effective realization of liberation; otherwise we would remain in the contradictory situation embodied in traditional beneficence, which required the presence of poor people so that virtue might be practiced. Right now theologians need captive peoples in order to be able to talk about the Gospel as liberation" (p. 210).

21. Francisco Vanderhoff, "La epistemología moderna y la problemética teológica actual," in *Liberación y cautiverio,* p. 289.

22. Gustavo Gutiérrez, "Por una teología y una liturgia de la liberación," *Liaisons Internationales* (Bulletin 10 [Aug.–Sept. 1975], pp. 10ff.), identi-

fies the "poor" of the Gospel with those he prefers to call "non-persons" (p. 11). It is these people who must be the starting point for theology (p. 12). They are the ones who are to proclaim the word of God: "Only in association with him [the non-person] can we carry on the work of theological reflection." The non-person is the theological source par excellence.

23. Cf. Pablo Richard, "Teología de la liberación latinoamericana," *Liaisons Internationales,* Bulletin 8 (Jan.–Feb. 1975), p. 21.

24. See the article cited in n. 18 (p. 49).

25. Vanderhoff, *art. cit.* (n. 21, above), p. 289.

26. Raúl Vidales, "Acotaciones a la problemática sobre el método en la Teología de la Liberación," in *Liberación y cautiverio,* p. 257.

27. Vanderhoff and Campos, *art. cit.* (n. 18, above), p. 52).

28. On the meaning of the word "ideology" as used by Christians for socialism, cf. Ricardo Alberdi, "Opción de clase y acceso a la verdad," *Iglesia Viva* (1975), pp. 535–57, esp. pp. 540–42; Jacques Sommet, "Marxismo, ciencia y ideología," *Iglesia Viva* (1974), esp. pp. 394ff.; Alberto Alzate P., "El encubrimiento como arma ideológica," *Franciscanum* (Bogotá, 1976), pp. 169–237.

29. Gustavo Gutiérrez at the workshop on "participación de los cristianos en la construcción del socialismo en Chile," April 1971; published in *Cristianos Latinoamericanos y Socialismo* (Bogotá: CEDIAL, 1972), p. 28.

30. Pablo Richard, *Cristianismo, Lucha Ideológica y Racionalidad Histórica* (Salamanca: Sígueme, 1975), p. 21.

31. Statement published in *Los Cristianos y el Socialismo* (Buenos Aires: Siglo Veintiuno, 1973), pp. 115–21; text cited on p. 121. Translated by John Drury in John Eagleson (ed.), *Christians for Socialism: Documentation of the Christians for Socialism Movement in Latin America* (Maryknoll, N.Y.: Orbis, 1975), p. 140.

32. Pierre Bigo S.J., "Nuevo documento de los Cristianos por Socialismo," *Medellín,* 2 (1976): 41.

33. Gutiérrez, *art. cit.* (n. 22, above), p. 13.

34. Cf. n. 6, above, Page references in the text are from this translation.

35. *Art. cit.* (n. 23, above), p. 21.

36. Vidales, *art. cit.* (n. 26, above), pp. 258–59.

37. Mario Peresson S.D.B., in his lecture in a series of conferences on faith and politics, April 1976; text distributed by the SAL group of Bogotá.

38. For an example of this zeal to "Latin-americanize," see the theses proposed by Ignacio Ellacuría S.J., "Posibildad, necesidad y sentido de una teología latinoamericana," *Christus* (Mexico City), February 1976, pp. 12–16; cf. March 1976, pp. 17–23. Ellacuría speaks constantly of a "Latin American theology," but it is impossible to pin this theology down. What he calls "Latin American theology" seems to be something he himself has excogitated. Instead of saying "I think," he says "Latin American theology

thinks"; frequently, instead of "Latin American theology," he might have said "Karl Rahner S.J.," since many of the theses he presents as "Latin American" are simply opinions of Karl Rahner. In thesis 9.7.3 he says: "Latin American Christology attributes exceptional importance to the events of Jesus' life as a primary locus of God's communication with man." Such a statement is not "Latin American" but simply "Catholic." The same must be said of thesis 10.2.1: "What bothers Latin American theology is not the magisterium but an uncritical reading of the magisterium and a denial of personal responsibility for theory by a mechanical repetition of the same statements." In fact, this bothers not only Latin American theology but theology in every form. Ellacuría's anxiety to "Latin-americanize" shows in other theses too, for example, thesis 6.5.2: "Not all essential theological topics have as yet been handled in a Latin American manner," or thesis 6.4.4: "Latin American theology does not accept the idea of explaining the relation between the divine and the human in terms of nature and supernature." Who refuses to accept it? Everyone? Or only Fr. Ignacio Ellacuría?

39. Jon Sobrino S.J., "El conocimiento teológico el la teología europea y latinoamericana," in *Liberación y Cautiverio,* pp. 177–207; citations are from p. 191.

40. Cf. the text of the workshop in Richard, *Cristianos por el Socialismo,* pp. 272–76; citation is from p. 273.

41. In his *Cristianismo, Lucha Ideológica y Racionalidad Histórica* (n. 30, above), p. 20.

42. Cf. n. 37, above.

43. "Catequesis del acontecimiento," *Cursos de Iglesia y Vocación* (Bogotá), no. 67 (Jan.–Feb. 1971), pp. 1–6.

44. No. 146 (Oct.–Dec. 1976), pp. 20–30 (published at Bogotá).

45. In Eagleson (e.), *Christians for Socialism,* p. 174.

46. Esteban Torres, "Búsqueda de Dios en la lucha política liberadora," *Contacto* (Dec. 1975), p. 43.

47. Estella (Navarre): Editorial Verbo Divino, 1975. 451 pp.

48. Cf. Jesús Delgado, "Lectura latinoamericana del Evangelio de San Marcos," *Estudios Centroamericanos* (El Salvador) (Aug.–Sept. 1975), pp. 532–54.

49. Bogotá: Ediciones Tercer Mundo, 1976.

50. XXXIInd Plenary Assembly, *Identidad Cristiana en la Acción por la Justicia* (Bogotá: SPEC, 1976), no. 39.

51. *Oración desde la Praxis Liberadora,* in the series Estudios Encuentro, nos. 3–4. 220 pp.

52. Report in *Los Cristianos y el Socialismo* (Buenos Aires: Siglo Veintiuno, 1973), p. 117; in Eagleson (ed.), *Christians for Socialism,* pp. 137–38.

53. *Op. cit.,* p. 165.

54. Cf. the Avila document (no. 16 in the list), nos. 38–41; Rafael

Belda, "Los Cristianos por el Socialismo ante el ateísmo Marxista," *Iglesia Viva* (1974), pp. 401–16; Giulio Girardi, "Los cristianos de hoy ante el Marxismo," *Iglesia Viva* (1974), pp. 325–54.

55. Pope Paul VI, *Evangelii nuntiandi*, no. 27, in *TPS*, 21 (1976): 16.

56. In Eagleson, *op. cit.*, p. 214.

57. In his *Cristianos por el Socialismo*, p. 204.

58. *Hebdo* 76/26, p. 5.

59. *Op. cit.*, p. 203; italics in the original.

60. Text in *Cristianos Latinoamericanos y Socialismo* (Bogotá: CEDIAL, 1972), pp. 191–200.

61. Text in Bulletin 4 (Sept. 1974) of the SAL group of Medellín, p. 3 (italics in the original).

62. This is also the task of the various Commissions for Justice and Peace, which have the support of the Vatican.

63. In *Medellín*, 2 (1976): 478–79.

64. *The Church in the Present Day Transformation of Latin America in the Light of the Council*, ed. L. M. Colonnese (Bogotá: General Secretariat of the Latin American Episcopal Conference, 1970), vol. 2: *Conclusions*, "Statement on Peace," no. 1 (p. 71).

65. *Op. cit.*, nos. 2 and 14a (pp. 71 and 76).

66. This is document 10 in our list; text in Richard, *Cristianos por el Socialismo*, p. 256. Here is the cited text in its context: "CfS is an assemblage of Christians who may or may not be militants in the various leftist parties but are committed to the working class and its struggle for socialism. These Christians adopt the Marxist analysis as their own, and make it their immediate objective to collaborate in the takeover of power by the working class. CfS provides a platform for denouncing social Christianity and groups that use Christianity in order to oppress the people. CfS shows by their deeds that being a Christian and being a revolutionary are not incompatible. In addition, CfS makes a contribution to revolutionary unity, without thereby blessing parties or governments. Finally, CfS brings together Christians who seek to live their faith in a revolutionary way."

In his *A Theology of Liberation* (pp. 272–79), Gustavo Gutiérrez openly defends the class struggle. He accepts "the division of humanity into oppressors and oppressed" (p. 273); he states that "the class struggle is a fact, and neutrality in this matter is impossible," even though "the class struggle poses problems to the universality of Christian love" (ibid.); he thinks that "to build a just society necessarily implies the active and conscious participation in the class struggle that is occurring before our eyes" (p. 274); he repeats that neutrality is impossible and that "when the Church rejects the class struggle, it is objectively operating as a part of the prevailing system" (p. 275). To resolve the difficulty the class struggle entails for the universality of Christian love, he grants that we must love our enemies, that is, the oppressors, but observes that "one loves the oppressors by liberating them from their inhuman condition as oppressors, by liberating them from themselves . . . by combatting the oppressive class" (p. 276). He cites Girardi: "We love the oppressors by fighting them" (p. 285, n. 56), and adds: "It must be a real and effective combat, not hate" (p. 276).

Combat them *without hating them!* But is a class struggle without hatred really possible? Che Guevara, the idol of the Latin American revolutionaries, wrote in his "political testament": "Hatred as a factor in struggle; intransigent hatred of the enemy, which drives a man beyond his natural limitations and begets effective violence, turning the man into a selective, cold machine for killing. That is what our soldiers must be like; a people that does not hate cannot triumph over a brutal enemy" (cited by Francisco Interdonato, "Desacralizar la lucha de clases en la teología latinoamericana," *Revista Teológica Limense* [1976], p. 16).

In Gutiérrez' view, moreover, to speak of the priest as "the man of unity" is to try to make him a part of the prevailing system (p. 277).

It is clear that throughout this discussion the concept of oppressor needs clarification. In the eyes of the CfS, all those who are not poor or who do not make a "class option" in favor of the poor against the rich are simply "oppressors" and therefore "enemies" who must be combated. In this sense, by rejecting the class struggle the Church becomes an "oppressor" and an "enemy." Gutiérrez says: "In the context of the class struggle today, to love one's enemies presupposes recognizing and accepting that one has class enemies and that it is necessary to combat them" (p. 276). The Church, then, is an assembly of "enemies."

Raúl Vidales, a faithful partisan of his friend Gustavo Gutiérrez, has announced a great discovery: "We now see clearly that to leave the Gospel above and outside the class struggle is to reduce it to an ideology that in the last analysis legitimizes the established order" (in *Liberación y Cautiverio,* p. 220).

67. From a letter of Cardinal Amleto Cicognani. See my study of Christian salvation and man's temporal progress as presented in the teaching of the Second General Conference of the Latin American Episcopate (Medellín, 1968), in *Medellín,* 2 (1976): 62–73.

68. Statement at the Latin American Theological Conference, Mexico City, August 1976; cf. *Liberación y Cautiverio,* pp. 546–47.

69. Comblin, *art. cit.,* p. 546.

70. "Condicionamientos actuales de la reflexión teológica en Latinoamerica," in *Liberación y Cautiverio,* pp. 91–101.

71. See his address to "the Eighty" in April 1971 on Marxism and Christianity; text in *Cristianos Latinoamericanos y Socialismo* (Bogotá: CEDIAL, 1972), pp. 15–35.

72. *Cristianos por el Socialismo,* p. 206.

73. Text published in *Servicio Colombiano de Comunicación Social* (Bogotá, May 1976).

74. Synod of Bishops (1971), *Justice in the World,* pt. II, in *TPS,* 16 (1971–72): 382.

75. *Evangelii nuntiandi,* no. 76, in *TPS,* 21 (1976): 44.

76. *The Theological Formation of Future Priests* (Feb. 22, 1976), no. 39, in *TPS,* 21 (1976): 351.

77. Vatican Council I, *Dogmatic Constitution on the Catholic Faith (Dei Filius),* chap. 3; text in Henry Denzinger and Adolf Schönmetzer (eds.), *Enchiridion symbolorum* (32nd ed.; Freiburg, 1963), no. 3016 (older editions, no. 1796). (Henceforth *DS,* with number of text.)

78. For a detailed discussion of praxis in theology see John Duns Scotus' *Opus oxoniense* (or *Ordinatio*), Gonzalo of Balboa's *Quaestiones disputatae,* the work of St. Anthony of Lisbon, and the work of St. Bonaventure, among others.

79. *Art cit.* (n. 18, above), p. 50.

80. Pope Paul VI, *Evangelii nuntiandi,* no. 35, in *TPS,* 21 (1976): 19.

81. "Introduction aux Béatitudes," *Nouvelle revue théologique,* 98 (1976): 104.

82. "Teología bíblica de la liberación," in *Conversaciones de Toledo* (Toledo: Ediciones de Aldecoa, 1974), pp. 152ff.

83. Council of Trent, session 6, *Decree on Justification,* chap. 3 (*DS,* no. 1523; older editions, no. 795).

84. *Sermo* 344, 4 (*PL,* 39:1515).

85. The text of this fine letter is in Vekemans, *op. cit.,* pp. 372–77; citation is from p. 373.

86. Segundo Galilea, *Teología de la Liberación: Ensayo de síntesis* (Bogotá: Indo-American Service, 1976).

87. Pope Paul VI, *Evangelii nuntiandi,* nos. 35–36, in *TPS,* 21 (1976): 19–20.

Appendix

1. There was, of course, another "final document": a "dry list" of 67 questions that were discussed during the Synod. And on October 23 the Fathers were surprised to be handed a statement, "Human Rights and Reconciliation," which had not been previously studied, much less discussed; it was simply read, immediately approved by a show of hands, and published.

2. Apostolic Letter (motu proprio), *Apostolica sollicitudo* (Sept. 15, 1965); translated in *TPS,* 10 (1964–65) 340.

3. Address, *Ecce ad Nostrae* (Oct. 26, 1974), in *TPS,* 19 (1974–75) 198.

4. The documents I have before me are the following:

1) A document on Evangelization in the Modern World, produced by the secretariat of the Synod for the use of the episcopal conferences and

sent to them in May 1973; also known as *Lineamenta* or *Outline.* 24 printed pages.

2) The responses of the episcopal conferences to the *Outline,* of which I have only the responses of the Latin American Episcopal Conference (published in *CELAM,* no. 80, 20 pp.), of the Brazilian bishops (published in *Comunicado Mensual,* no. 263), of the Italian bishops (published in the collection *Documenti CEI,* no. 10), of the Spanish bishops, and of the Commission for Justice and Peace. I also have a copy of the report drawn up by the synodal secretariat on all the responses of the episcopal conferences.

3) The *Instrumentum Laboris* or *Working Paper,* redacted by the synodal secretariat in 1974. 24 pages.

4) The opening address of Pope Paul VI, in *TPS,* 19 (1974–75) 185–92.

5) The *Panorama,* a "picture" of the situation in the Church since the Synod of 1971. The *Panorama* was ordered by Paul VI, based on reports requested for the purpose from the episcopal conferences of the world, and composed, at the Pope's request, by Cardinal Aloisio Lorscheider, president of the Brazilian Episcopal Conference.

6) Five reports that served as an introduction to the first part of the synodal discussion, that is, the discussion of the bishops' experiences in the area of evangelization. The five reports included a report on Africa, by Bishop James Sangu of Meyba, Tanzania; a report on Latin America, by Bishop Eduardo Pironio of Mar del Plata, Argentina; a report on North America, Australia, and Oceania, by Bishop Joseph Bernardin, archbishop of Cincinnati, U.S.A.; a report on Asia, by Cardinal Joseph Cordeiro, archbishop of Karachi, Pakistan; and a report on Europe, by Bishop Roger Etchegaray, archbishop of Marseilles, France.

7) The 109 addresses (oral or written) on the first part of the synodal discussion, that is, on the shared experiences of evangelization. I have a photocopy of all of these.

8) The report made at the end of this first part by Cardinal Joseph Cordeiro. This report was intended to sum up the addresses of the bishops and to be a transition to the discussion in smaller groups that were divided according to language area (cf. n. 12, below). This report is a very valuable document of 43 printed pages.

9) The reports of the 12 language groups, which also are valuable. I have a photocopy of these.

10) The addresses made after the presentation of reports by the language groups. A total of 18 documents, in photocopy.

11) The report with which Cardinal Karol Wojtyla introduced the second part of the discussion, that is, the discussion of the theological problems raised by the experiences discussed in the first part. 31 printed pages.

12) The 169 (oral or written) addresses on this second part. I have a photocopy of all.

13) Cardinal Wojtyla's report concluding this second part of the general discussion and leading to the discussion in language groups. 28 printed pages.

14) Reports of the 12 language groups. A valuable set of documents, of which I have a photocopy.

15) The intervention, or addresses, made after the presentation of the group reports. There are 58 of them, many delivered only in writing. I have a photocopy of all.

16) Draft of a first final declaration, in four sections (41 printed pp.), rejected in a test vote.

17) "Human Rights and Reconciliation" statement, in *TPS,* 19 (1974–75) 216–19.

18) The 205 *modi*, or emendations, suggested for the final statement. I have a photocopy of these.

19) The final declaration; in *TPS,* 19 (1974–75) 229–34.

20) The list of the questions discussed at the Synod.

21) Closing address of Pope Paul VI; in *TPS,* 19 (1974–75) 192–99.

All this is a documentation that is rich in content, but the various documents are not of equal value. An address that represents a bishop's personal views cannot be placed on a par with an address in the name of an episcopal conference. But even among the latter, we must distinguish between episcopal conferences with many members (Brazil, e.g., has 250 bishops) and those with few (Honduras, Costa Rica, and Panama have 7 bishops). A report is more important than an address, etc. In his closing discourse, Pope Paul VI said: "Not everything that emerged is to be regarded as valid. Some points that were legitimately stressed require modification in details. Others, especially those made by the discussion groups, require sharper definition, qualification, completion and further study" (*TPS,* 19 [1974–75] 196). Among the examples he gives of such points, he mentions what was said about liberation and its connection with evangelization.

5. *TPS,* 19 (1974–75) 232–33.

6. Cf. Juan Alfaro S.J., *Cristianismo y Justicia* (Madrid: Ediciones PPC, 1973), p. 5. This book is no. 3 in a series that is being published by the Commission for Justice and Peace.

7. Synod of Bishops, 1971, *Justice in the World,* in *TPS,* 16 (1971–72) 377.

8. Pope Paul VI, address, *Postquam liturgicum,* at the opening of the Synod of 1974 (Sept. 27, 1974), in *TPS,* 19 (1974–75) 189.

9. All of my citations from the cardinals, archbishops, bishops, and other Fathers of the Synod are taken from their oral or written addresses during the Synod, unless I specify that a report is the source.

10. Cf. Alfaro, op. cit., p. 38.

11. *Justice in the World,* in *TPS,* 16 (1971–72) 382.

12. French Group B (II). The discussions of the Synod were on two successive subjects: (1) sharing of experiences with regard to evangeliza-

tion and (2) theological problems implicit in these experiences. After general discussion of each, further discussion was carried on within 12 language groups. Speakers of English, French, and Spanish or Portuguese (the Portuguese were more or less lumped with the Spanish and given a group of their own) were subdivided into three groups (A, B, and C). Thus "French Group B (II)" means the second of the three French-speaking groups in its discussion of the second major topic, that is, theological problems implicit in their experiences of evangelization.

13. "Un gozo incontenibile," homily at the closing mass of the Latin American bishops' meeting (Nov. 3, 1974), in *Osservatore Romano,* Nov. 4–5, 1974.

14. On the necessity, in some situations, of "silent witness," Spanish-Portuguese Group A (II) offered these thoughts: "Pedagogical adaptation to the recipient, as well as the special difficulties encountered in some environments, require that in some cases the reference to Christ be tacit, implicit, and circumspect. Frequently, any explicit reference must be preceded by an individual or collective witness of faith and love, and this witness must at the present time take the form of helping the peoples develop. We recognize and appreciate the importance of this silent witness in the form of a simple Christian presence in these environments, and the sacrifice such an approach requires of these Christians, especially of such as work in science or the arts, where an explicit witness to the faith is not possible. Every work of human development, when it proceeds from apostolic concern, is an action inspired by the Holy Spirit and therefore a genuinely evangelizing action. The proclamation of the Gospel message purifies and makes use of many values and aspirations of the people being evangelized. An indispensable condition of such a Christian presence is profound love, a heartfelt empathy for individuals, respect for the stages a people must pass through in its maturation, and collaboration on the great human problems of peace, justice, culture, and the common good. At the same time, the essential goal of all evangelizing action must be to invite men to faith in Jesus Christ or to help them live in accordance with this faith. This is always possible, at least in personal contacts and when a suitable occasion offers."

15. Homily at the closing Mass of the Latin American bishops' meeting (cf. n. 13, above).

16. *TPS,* 19 (1974–75) 190.

17. Ibid., p. 194.

18. Ibid., pp. 216–17 (italics added).

19. *TPS,* 16 (1971–72) 383.

20. *TPS,* 19 (1974–75) 197.

21. This statement must be qualified, however, by saying that "popular theology" reflected this view more often than did the classical theologians.

22. Cf. "Algunos aspectos de la evangelización en América Latina"

(points for reflection submitted by the Latin American Episcopal Conference to the coming Synod of Bishops), *CELAM,* March 1974, p. 12.

23. GS 24c/223.
24. See n. 13, above.
25. Ibid.
26. *Populorum progressio* (Mar. 26, 1967), no. 6, in *TPS,* 12 (1967) 146.
27. *Populorum progressio,* no. 15, in *TPS,* 12 (1967) 149.
28. The pre-synodal report of the Spanish episcopate calls attention to the countless specific ways of helping the neighbor (in the temporal order) that must be undertaken immediately, according to the possibilities available to each individual. "At times the legitimate desire for a radical transformation of social structures serves many as an excuse for not accomplishing the more modest good which each individual can do for his brothers in everyday life and which all of us are duty-bound to do according to our ability." Bishop Alfonso López, secretary general of the Conference of Latin American Bishops, said at the Synod: "Not one but a great many bishops, not one but a great many priests, religious, and lay persons are fighting the battle of Christ where Christian witness is more difficult and requires greater self-sacrifice; they act in unsensational ways and without waving flags; they sow the seed in joy, simplicity, and silence."

DATE DUE

OCT 15 '88			
APR 13 '97			
DE 19 '98			
DE 13 '01			